Within th

Why This Book Matters Now

We find ourselves at a pivotal moment in history—a juncture marked by uncertainty, rapid change, and a palpable sense of disillusionment among the younger generation. The Fourth Turning, a concept introduced by historians William Strauss and Neil Howe, posits that society undergoes a cyclical process of transformation every eighty to one hundred years, culminating in a crisis that fundamentally alters the social and political landscape. As we navigate this turbulent period, it becomes increasingly clear that the challenges we face are not merely economic or political in nature but are deeply rooted in the shifting sands of cultural and generational dynamics.

This book matters now more than ever because it addresses the growing sense of hopelessness and disillusionment that has taken hold among young people. From the seemingly insurmountable barriers to homeownership and career advancement to the pervasive feeling that hard work no longer guarantees success, the current generation is facing a crisis of faith in the very institutions that once promised stability and prosperity. This disillusionment, if left unaddressed, is a recipe for disaster, threatening to unravel the social fabric that binds us together.

Moreover, the book is a call to action, urging readers to confront the realities of the Fourth Turning head-on and to consider the role that each of us can play in shaping a more hopeful and equitable future. Through a careful examination of historical patterns, current socio-economic trends, and the lived experiences of individuals across the globe, we aim to inspire a reimagining of success, community, and collective well-being in the face of mounting challenges.

In essence, this book is an invitation to engage with the critical issues of our time—to question, to reflect, and ultimately, to envision a path forward that honors the complexity and potential of the human spirit. By understanding where we stand in the cycle of historical turnings, we can begin to chart a course that leads us out of disillusionment and toward a future characterized by resilience, innovation, and a renewed sense of purpose.

Table of Contents

Preface
- Why This Book Matters Now

Part I: Understanding the Fourth Turning

1. The Nature of Historical Cycles
   - The Theory of the Fourth Turning: Origins and Overview
   - The Rhythms of History: A Pattern of Rebirth and Decline
   - Identifying the Turnings: From High to Crisis

2. The Fourth Turning in Context
   - Signs of the Times: How We Know We're in a Fourth Turning
   - Historical Examples of Fourth Turnings
   - The Global Perspective: Fourth Turnings Beyond the West

Part II: The Current Crisis

3. Economic Foundations of Despair
   - The Elusive Dream of Home Ownership
   - The Gig Economy and Precarious Work
   - The Student Debt Quagmire and Education's Broken Promise

4. Social and Psychological Dimensions

- The Mental Health Epidemic: Anxiety, Depression, and Beyond
- The Disillusionment with Institutions: Government, Media, and Corporations
- The Crisis of Meaning: Searching for Purpose in a Material World

5. Technological Ties that Bind and Isolate
   - Digital Life: Connection or Isolation?
   - The Impact of Social Media on Self-Esteem and Reality Perception
   - Automation and the Future of Work: An Uncertain Path

Part III: The Generation at the Heart

6. A Portrait of a Generation
   - Defining the Generational Cohorts: Who Are They?
   - Values, Hopes, and Fears: What Matters to Them
   - The Role of Education: Shaping or Misshaping Futures?

7. Disconnected Communities
   - The Erosion of Local Communities and Its Impacts
   - The Rise of Virtual Communities: A New Form of Belonging?
   - The Decline of Civic Engagement and Its Consequences

Part IV: Precursors to Disaster

8. Historical Lessons and Modern Parallels
   - Societal Upheaval: From the French Revolution to the 1960s
   - Economic Disasters and Their Aftermath: The Great Depression and 2008 Financial Crisis
   - The Warning Signs: What History Teaches Us About Today

9. The Politics of Discontent
   - Polarization and Radicalization: The Fuel of Conflict
   - The Rise of Populism and Nationalism: A Response to Disillusionment
   - The Danger of Ignoring the Middle: The Forgotten Majority

Part V: Toward Renewal

10. Redefining Success and Prosperity
    - Beyond GDP: New Measures of Societal Health and Success
    - The Case for a Universal Basic Income
    - Education Reimagined: Lifelong Learning and Adaptability

11. Building Resilient Communities
    - Grassroots Movements and Local Solutions
    - The Power of Social Capital: Rebuilding Trust and Engagement
    - Technology as a Tool for Good: Enhancing Rather Than Replacing Human Connections

12. The Role of Leadership in a Time of Crisis
    - Ethical Leadership: Steering Societies Through Stormy Seas
    - Bridging Divides: The Importance of Inclusive Politics
    - Youth Empowerment: Engaging the Next Generation in Shaping the Future

Epilogue: The Path Forward
- Lessons Learned and the Road Ahead
- A Call to Action for All Generations

<u>Hard times create strong men, strong men create good times, good times create weak men, and weak men create hard times.</u>

Part I: Understanding the Fourth Turning

Chapter 1: The Nature of Historical Cycles

This chapter looks into the cyclical nature of history, exploring the theory of the Fourth Turning and its implications for understanding the patterns of societal change. Through a detailed examination of historical cycles, we aim to provide readers with the tools necessary to recognize the signs and stages of these cycles, offering insight into the current era and its challenges.

<u>The Theory of the Fourth Turning: Origins and Overview</u>

The Fourth Turning theory, as proposed by William Strauss and Neil Howe in their seminal work, posits that societal time can be divided into cycles of approximately 80-100 years, each comprising four turnings or phases: the High, the Awakening, the Unraveling, and the Crisis. These cycles, known as saecula, echo the natural rhythms of human life, reflecting the generational shifts in attitudes, values, and behaviors that drive the evolution of society.

The origins of the Fourth Turning theory can be traced back to the observation of historical patterns that repeat themselves in a predictable manner. Strauss and Howe's analysis draws upon a wide array of historical sources, from ancient texts to modern data, to construct a framework that captures the essence of these recurring cycles. At the heart of their theory is the idea that each turning plays a distinct role in the lifecycle of a society, shaping the collective experience of its members and setting the stage for the next phase of development.

The Rhythms of History: A Pattern of Rebirth and Decline

The cyclical view of history suggests that societies undergo a process of rebirth and decline, moving through periods of growth, maturation, entropy, and regeneration. This perspective challenges linear interpretations of history, emphasizing instead the dynamic interplay between order and chaos, stability and transformation.

At the core of this cyclical process is the intergenerational transmission of values, knowledge, and social norms. Each generation, shaped by the prevailing conditions of its formative years, responds to the challenges and opportunities of its era in ways that leave an indelible mark on the course of history. The rhythms of history are thus a reflection of the collective journey of humanity, a dance of progress and retreat that unfolds over centuries.

Identifying the Turnings: From High to Crisis

The four turnings that constitute a saeculum are characterized by distinct social moods, public behaviors, and institutional configurations. Understanding these turnings is crucial for interpreting the signals of change and anticipating the challenges and opportunities that lie ahead.

1. The High (The First Turning): A period of societal consolidation and agreement on core values, often following a crisis. This phase is marked by strong institutions, a sense of collective purpose, and an optimistic outlook on the future.

2. The Awakening (The Second Turning): A time of spiritual renewal and challenge to established norms, characterized by a shift towards individualism and a questioning of societal values. This turning often features a cultural or religious revival, alongside growing tensions between older and younger generations.

3. The Unraveling (The Third Turning): During this phase, institutions weaken, and individualism flourishes, leading to a fragmentation of societal consensus. The unraveling is marked by a growing sense of disenchantment with established authority and a rise in cynicism and self-interest.

4. The Crisis (The Fourth Turning): The culmination of the cycle, a crisis is a period of upheaval and renewal, where society confronts existential threats and is forced to redefine its very identity. This turning is characterized by dramatic changes in social structures, a reinvigoration of community, and the emergence of a new social order.

By examining the characteristics and dynamics of each turning, we can gain insights into the forces that shape historical change and better understand the challenges and possibilities of the Fourth Turning. Through this analysis, the nature of historical cycles is revealed as a powerful lens through which to view the past, navigate the present, and anticipate the future.

Chapter 2: The Fourth Turning in Context

This chapter looks deeper into the current Fourth Turning, offering a comprehensive analysis of its signs, historical precedents, and its global implications. By examining the evidence and comparing past cycles, we aim to provide a nuanced understanding of how these dynamics manifest globally, transcending cultural and geographical boundaries.

Signs of the Times: How We Know We're in a Fourth Turning

The Fourth Turning, characterized by widespread societal upheaval and the reconfiguration of social, economic, and political structures, is identifiable through various signs that signal its onset. These indicators not only highlight the turmoil inherent to this phase but also underscore the transformative potential that lies within it.

1. Economic Instabilities and Crises: The onset of the Fourth Turning is often heralded by significant economic challenges, including financial crises, severe recessions, and the destabilization of longstanding economic systems and practices. Such disruptions provoke a reevaluation of economic policies and the societal values underpinning them.

2. Political Polarization and Renewal: A marked increase in political polarization, characterized by the emergence of extremist ideologies and a breakdown in bipartisan cooperation, signals the deep societal divisions that define the Fourth Turning. This period also witnesses the call for political renewal, with movements demanding systemic change gaining momentum.

3. Social Unrest and Movements for Change: Widespread social unrest, driven by a demand for justice, equity, and systemic reform, characterizes this phase. From protests against economic inequality to movements advocating for social justice, the Fourth Turning is a period of active engagement and societal redefinition.

4. Technological and Environmental Shifts: Significant technological advancements, alongside acute environmental crises, challenge existing societal models and necessitate new ways of thinking and living. These shifts contribute to the broader sense of uncertainty and opportunity that defines the Fourth Turning.

Historical Examples of Fourth Turnings

Examining past Fourth Turnings provides valuable insights into the patterns and outcomes of these transformative periods. Each historical example sheds light on the challenges faced and the changes enacted, offering lessons for navigating the current cycle.

1. The American Revolution (1770s-1790s): This period redefined the identity and governance of the American colonies, leading to the establishment of a new nation based on principles of democracy and liberty.

2. The Civil War (1860s): A profound conflict that resolved the festering issue of slavery, leading to the reunification of the United States and significant amendments to the Constitution, fundamentally altering the nation's social fabric.

3. The Great Depression and World War II (1930s-1940s): These crises reshaped the global order and domestic policies, leading to the creation of the welfare state, the rise of the United States as a superpower, and the establishment of international institutions designed to prevent future conflicts.

The Global Perspective: Fourth Turnings Beyond the West

While the concept of the Fourth Turning has been primarily analyzed through the lens of Western history, similar cycles of upheaval and renewal can be observed in other cultures and regions. This global perspective highlights the universality of cyclical historical patterns, albeit manifested in diverse contexts.

1. The Meiji Restoration in Japan (1860s-1880s): A period of rapid modernization and societal transformation, which saw the consolidation of imperial power and the integration of Western technologies and institutions, fundamentally altering Japan's trajectory.

2. The Xinhai Revolution in China (1911-1912): Marked the end of imperial rule in China and the establishment of the Republic of

China, initiating a period of profound social, political, and cultural change.

3. Post-Colonial Transformations: Many countries undergoing decolonization in the mid-20th century experienced their own form of a Fourth Turning, as they sought to redefine their national identities, governance structures, and place in the world order following the end of colonial rule.

These examples underscore the Fourth Turning's global relevance, demonstrating how periods of crisis and renewal are pivotal moments that reshape societies in fundamental ways, regardless of geographical or cultural differences. Understanding these dynamics offers valuable insights into the nature of change and the potential pathways toward a more resilient and equitable global society.

Part II: The Current Crisis

Chapter 3: Economic Foundations of Despair

In today's era, a profound sense of despair blankets many, especially the younger demographics. This malaise is not arbitrary but rooted in significant economic transformations that starkly contrast the realities faced by prior generations. The pursuit of homeownership, once a hallmark of success and stability, has become a distant dream for many. The job market, increasingly dominated by the gig economy, offers precarious work arrangements that lack the security and benefits of traditional employment. Simultaneously, the dream of higher education has morphed into a nightmare of debt for countless students, with the promised return on investment slipping further away. Together, these economic phenomena have created a tapestry of instability and shattered expectations, setting the stage for widespread disillusionment and anxiety.

The Elusive Dream of Home Ownership

The American Dream, encapsulated in the idea of owning a home, has symbolized success, stability, and security for generations. However, this dream is increasingly out of reach for many Americans, particularly younger adults and middle-class families. A historical overview reveals that post-World War II policies and economic conditions favored homeownership, making it an accessible goal for many Americans. However, recent decades have witnessed a dramatic shift. The convergence of rapid urbanization, a constrained housing supply, and the financialization of real estate has led to soaring real estate prices, rendering the housing market dauntingly inaccessible.

In this context, the alterations in housing affordability and economic conditions have precipitated profound social and psychological consequences, not merely altering market dynamics but reshaping the fabric of society itself. The aspiration for homeownership, once a cornerstone of personal achievement and stability, has been relegated to the realm of the elusive for many, exacerbating the divide between socioeconomic classes. This widening chasm not only undermines the middle class but also engenders a societal landscape marked by economic disparity.

The ramifications of these shifts are far-reaching, influencing family dynamics, housing stability, and individual well-being. The chapter delves into how the economic barriers to homeownership have led to postponed milestones in personal lives, such as marriage and childbearing. The trend towards delayed family formation is a reflection of the broader uncertainties and financial pressures facing younger generations, for whom the accumulation of wealth necessary for such commitments has become increasingly challenging.

The pivot towards rental housing emerges as a significant trend, underscoring the changing perceptions of housing as a means to wealth and stability. This shift not only reflects the adaptability of individuals in the face of economic constraints but also highlights the growing precariousness of housing security. As more individuals and families find themselves reliant on the rental market, issues of affordability, tenants' rights, and housing quality come to the forefront, demanding attention from policymakers and communities alike.

The psychological ramifications of these economic and social shifts are profound. The perception of stagnation, where upward mobility seems out of reach for many, fosters feelings of disillusionment and disenfranchisement. The psychological toll of living in a society where economic advancement appears increasingly unattainable cannot be overstated. It affects not only individual mental health but also the social cohesion and resilience of communities.

This underscores the necessity of understanding these complex interrelations between economic changes, social dynamics, and psychological well-being. By examining the consequences of the housing market's evolution, it calls for a reevaluation of the values and policies that guide our societies, advocating for measures that ensure greater equity, stability, and opportunity for all citizens.

The Gig Economy and Precarious Work

The labor market has undergone a significant transformation with the rise of the gig economy. This new paradigm of work is characterized by flexibility and independence but also brings about precarity and instability. The gig economy, while innovative, lacks the traditional safeguards that have protected workers for decades, such as stable income, healthcare benefits, and retirement plans. This section delves into the dichotomy of the gig economy: its potential for creating new opportunities and its role in undermining job security and worker benefits.

As younger generations navigate the evolving economic terrain, they encounter a job market dramatically different from that of their predecessors. The once-reliable promises of job security, predictable career paths, and comprehensive benefits have faded, replaced by the rise of gig economy jobs, contract work, and fluctuating employment opportunities. This new landscape is marked by its lack of stability and predictability, making long-term planning a challenge and often a gamble.

The shift toward precarious employment has far-reaching implications, extending beyond individual careers into the fabric of society. Traditional milestones of adulthood, such as purchasing a home, starting a family, or investing in retirement, have become increasingly elusive. The uncertainty inherent in the job market has prompted many to delay these significant life decisions, leading to a reshaping of societal norms and expectations around success and stability.

The consequences of this transformation are multifaceted, affecting not only economic but also social dynamics. The erosion of stable, well-compensated employment as a cornerstone of the middle class threatens to widen the gap between the affluent and the rest, undermining the principle of equitable opportunity. As job security becomes a relic of the past for many, a growing sense of economic and social disenfranchisement among younger generations challenges the very foundation of the social contract.

Addressing these changes requires a holistic approach, integrating policy innovation with a reevaluation of societal values. There is a pressing need for policies that provide robust support systems for those navigating this uncertain job market, including accessible education and training programs, comprehensive social safety nets, and employment policies that reflect the realities of the modern economy. Additionally, fostering a cultural shift towards valuing diverse career paths and recognizing the worth of stability and well-being over traditional markers of success could help mitigate the psychological and social strain imposed by economic instability.

In navigating these challenges, there is an opportunity to build a more inclusive and resilient economy. By acknowledging and adapting to the realities facing younger generations in the workforce, society can pave the way for a future that embraces economic diversity, supports stability and security for all, and fosters a sense of community and shared prosperity. This involves not only policy reforms but also a collective reimagining of what constitutes a fulfilling and successful life in an ever-changing economic landscape.

The burgeoning student debt crisis casts a long shadow over the American dream, challenging the longstanding narrative that education is the surest route to success and prosperity. As the gateway to opportunity, higher education was once heralded as a worthy investment in one's future. Yet, this ideal has been steadily eroded by the relentless upward spiral of tuition costs and the proliferation of aggressive lending practices. The transformation of higher education from an accessible public good into a high-stakes financial gamble has left countless graduates burdened with a debt load that far outweighs the economic benefits of their degrees.

The origins of this crisis are manifold, rooted in decades of policy decisions, economic shifts, and cultural attitudes towards education and debt. College tuition fees have skyrocketed at a rate that far outpaces inflation, driven by a complex web of factors including reduced state funding, administrative bloat, and an arms race of campus amenities. Concurrently, the financialization of student aid has transformed what was once a public service into a lucrative market for private lenders, marked by high interest rates and unforgiving repayment terms. This environment has fostered an unsustainable cycle where students, lured by the promise of a brighter future, are instead ensnared in a trap of financial obligations that can stifle their economic prospects for decades.

The ramifications of this crisis extend far beyond the balance sheets, deeply affecting the very fabric of society. Burdened by debt, many young adults find themselves postponing or altogether forgoing traditional markers of adulthood, such as homeownership, marriage, and starting a family. The financial strain limits career options, pushing individuals towards higher-paying, often less fulfilling jobs, in a desperate bid to stay afloat. Moreover, the specter of student debt exacerbates socioeconomic inequalities, disproportionately impacting marginalized communities and widening the gap between the haves and the have-nots.

This analysis calls into question the sustainability of a higher education system that operates on the backs of its students, profiting from their aspirations while offering increasingly uncertain returns. It underscores the urgent need for comprehensive reform, aimed at both curbing the spiraling costs of college and reimagining the value of a degree in the modern economy. Potential solutions range from increased state and federal funding for education, to the implementation of more equitable funding models, to the radical rethinking of credentialing systems.

Reforming higher education is not merely an economic imperative but a moral one, essential for restoring the promise of education as a ladder to success. By confronting the student debt crisis head-on, we can begin to dismantle the barriers that impede the potential of the next generation, fostering a society that values knowledge and opportunity over profit and indebtedness.

Chapter 4: Social and Psychological Dimensions

This chapter looks into the profound social and psychological impacts that underscore the current crisis, highlighting the mental health epidemic, widespread disillusionment with key institutions, and the pervasive search for meaning in a materialistic world. These dimensions are crucial for understanding the depth of the challenges faced by the current generation and the societal context of the Fourth Turning.

The Mental Health Epidemic: Anxiety, Depression, and Beyond

The rise of mental health issues, including anxiety, depression, and other psychological disorders, has become one of the most alarming signs of the times. This epidemic is not just a health crisis but a social one, reflecting deeper issues of isolation, stress, and uncertainty that pervade modern life. Several factors contribute to this trend, including the pressures of economic instability, social media's impact on self-esteem and body image, and the overall pace of modern life which often prioritizes productivity over well-being.

- Economic Stressors: The link between economic insecurity and mental health cannot be overstated. The pressures of finding and maintaining stable employment, coupled with rising living costs, create a fertile ground for anxiety and depression.

- Social Media and Comparison Culture: The pervasive influence of social media has introduced a new dimension to social comparison, exacerbating feelings of inadequacy and loneliness. The curated images of success and happiness often contrast sharply with the realities of individual lives, deepening the sense of failure and isolation.

- The Pace of Modern Life: The relentless pace and demands of contemporary life often leave little room for reflection, community building, or rest, contributing to a widespread sense of burnout and existential malaise.

The Disillusionment with Institutions: Government, Media, and Corporations

A key feature of the Fourth Turning is a profound disillusionment with institutions that traditionally held societal trust, including government, media, and corporations. This disillusionment stems from a perception of these entities as self-serving, corrupt, or disconnected from the needs and values of ordinary people.

- Government and Political Polarization: Increasing political polarization and the perception of governmental ineffectiveness in addressing key societal issues have eroded trust in political institutions. This disillusionment is fueled by scandals, perceived partisanship, and a failure to deliver on promises of progress and equality.

- Media Skepticism: The role of media in shaping public opinion and discourse has come under scrutiny, with accusations of bias, sensationalism, and a failure to provide objective or meaningful coverage. The proliferation of misinformation and echo chambers on social media exacerbates this issue, leading to a fragmented and skeptical public.

- Corporate Distrust: The perception of corporations prioritizing profits over ethical considerations, environmental sustainability, and worker welfare has contributed to a growing distrust in the corporate world. High-profile scandals and the widening gap between executive and worker compensation amplify these concerns.

The Crisis of Meaning: Searching for Purpose in a Material World

Amid economic uncertainties and social upheavals, a deeper existential crisis looms—a crisis of meaning. This crisis reflects a collective struggle to find purpose and fulfillment in a world that often seems to prioritize material success over spiritual or communal values.

- Materialism and Spiritual Emptiness: The relentless pursuit of material success—often measured by wealth, status, and consumption—leaves many feeling empty and unfulfilled. This emptiness speaks to a hunger for a deeper sense of purpose that transcends material wealth.

- The Search for Community and Connection: In a world where traditional community bonds have weakened, many individuals seek new forms of connection and belonging. This search often involves a quest for like-minded communities that share similar values and aspirations, whether in physical spaces or through digital platforms.

- Redefining Success: There is a growing movement to redefine success in more holistic terms, incorporating well-being, community engagement, and environmental sustainability into this vision. This shift reflects a desire to create a more balanced and meaningful life in the face of societal pressures and expectations.

The social and psychological dimensions of the current crisis reveal the complex interplay between individual experiences and broader societal trends. Understanding these dynamics is essential for addressing the root causes of the crisis and forging pathways toward healing and transformation.

Chapter 5: Technological Ties that Bind and Isolate

In an age where technology permeates every aspect of our lives, its dual role as both a connector and divider has become increasingly apparent. This chapter explores the complex relationship between technology and society, examining how digital platforms influence our sense of connection, self-esteem, and perceptions of reality, as well as the broader implications of automation on the future of work.

Digital Life: Connection or Isolation?

The digital revolution, marked by the rise of the internet and mobile technology, has fundamentally transformed human communication, knitting the global community closer through bits and bytes. This new era has birthed vast online communities and social networks, spaces where individuals, regardless of physical distance, can discover a sense of belonging and support. These platforms offer the promise of an interconnected world, where shared interests and identities transcend geographical boundaries, fostering unprecedented levels of engagement and understanding.

Yet, this hyper-connectedness harbors a paradox. In a world where digital interactions are ubiquitous, a counterintuitive trend emerges: a profound sense of isolation and loneliness pervading the fabric of modern society. The irony of the digital age is that, while technical connectivity reaches unprecedented heights, emotional and social connections often suffer. Research highlights a disturbing correlation between excessive use of digital devices and a decline in face-to-face interactions. This shift away from in-person socialization erodes traditional social bonds, leading to an increasing sense of alienation among many.

Investigate in the intricate dynamics of digital connectivity, probing the complex relationship between online engagement and real-world social cohesion. It explores how the tools and platforms designed to unite us across the digital expanse can also contribute to a fragmented sense of community. The constant barrage of notifications and the lure of virtual interactions can detract from the richness of direct human contact, leading to shallow exchanges that lack the depth and emotional resonance of face-to-face conversations.

The curated personas often presented on social media platforms can exacerbate feelings of inadequacy and isolation, as individuals compare their everyday lives to the highlight reels of others. This phenomenon, known as the "compare and despair" effect, can lead to a cycle of loneliness and disconnection, where the quest for digital validation supplants meaningful personal connections.

This exploration seeks to unpack the nuances of our digital existence, recognizing the dual nature of technology as both a bridge and a barrier to genuine human connection. In navigating this digital landscape, it is crucial to foster awareness of the ways in which technology shapes our social interactions and emotional well-being. By striking a balance between online engagement and real-world connections, we can harness the potential of digital tools to enhance, rather than undermine, our sense of community and belonging.

The Impact of Social Media on Self-Esteem and Reality Perception

The digital age has ushered in a new epoch where social media platforms dominate the landscape of communication and self-expression. With their algorithmically curated feeds, emphasis on visual perfection, and the currency of likes and followers, these platforms wield a profound influence on individual self-esteem and the collective perception of reality. Users are inundated with a relentless stream of idealized images, from the meticulously staged snapshots of daily life to the filtered vistas of travel and beauty. This barrage of perfection sets an unrealistic benchmark for normalcy and success, skewing perceptions and fostering a pervasive sense of inadequacy among its audience.

This impact is acutely felt by younger demographics, who find themselves entangled in the web of social comparison. The developmental stages of adolescence and young adulthood are marked by a quest for identity and belonging, making these individuals particularly vulnerable to the pressures exerted by social media. The constant juxtaposition against seemingly flawless lives can erode self-esteem, fueling feelings of exclusion and self-doubt. This dynamic is compounded by the quantifiable metrics of popularity and approval inherent to social platforms, where the number of likes or followers can be misinterpreted as a direct measure of personal value or social standing.

The phenomenon of online personas complicates the concept of authenticity. The distinction between one's online presence and offline reality becomes increasingly blurred, challenging our understanding of what it means to be genuine. Social media encourages the presentation of an idealized self, often at the expense of authenticity. This curated self-representation contributes to a distorted reality, where the lines between genuine and manufactured experiences are obscured, prompting users to question the authenticity of their own lives and those of others.

This section looks into the psychological ramifications of social media, shedding light on the intricate relationship between digital platforms and self-perception. It explores how the idealized and often unattainable standards propagated online can undermine self-esteem, distort reality, and complicate the pursuit of authenticity. By examining the challenges of maintaining a healthy self-image and a grounded sense of reality in a hyper-connected world, this analysis underscores the need for critical media literacy and a mindful approach to social media engagement, aiming to mitigate its psychological toll and foster a healthier digital environment.

Automation and the Future of Work: An Uncertain Path

The advent of automation and artificial intelligence (AI) heralds a transformative era in the realm of work, characterized by both unprecedented opportunities and daunting challenges. As machines become increasingly capable of performing tasks traditionally undertaken by humans, from manufacturing to customer service, the efficiency gains are undeniable. Automation offers the allure of increased productivity, reduced errors, and the liberation of humans from repetitive and physically taxing labor. However, this technological evolution brings with it a complex array of socio-economic implications that demand careful consideration.

The specter of job displacement looms large, with automation threatening to render certain roles and skill sets obsolete. The impact is not uniform, as some sectors face more immediate risks than others. Manufacturing, logistics, and administrative roles, for example, are particularly vulnerable to automation due to the routine nature of many of their tasks. The disruption to these sectors has the potential to displace large swathes of the workforce, challenging the traditional pathways to employment and upward mobility that have sustained the middle class.

Beyond individual job loss, the broader implications for economic inequality are significant. As automation favors capital over labor, there is a risk that the benefits of increased productivity will accrue disproportionately to those who own and control the technology. Without intentional policy interventions, this dynamic could exacerbate existing disparities, deepening the divide between the economic elite and the rest of society.

The transition to a more automated world, therefore, presents a critical juncture for policymakers, businesses, and individuals alike. Adapting to these changes requires a multifaceted approach that addresses the immediate challenges of workforce displacement while also leveraging the opportunities automation presents for enhancing human work and creating new jobs.

Strategies for navigating the future of work include investing in education and retraining programs to equip workers with the skills needed in an increasingly automated economy. Emphasis on STEM (science, technology, engineering, and mathematics) fields, along with digital literacy and soft skills such as creativity and problem-solving, can prepare the workforce for the jobs of tomorrow. Additionally, fostering a culture of lifelong learning and adaptability will be crucial for individuals to navigate the evolving labor market.

Policy measures such as universal basic income (UBI), enhanced social safety nets, and progressive taxation could also play a role in mitigating the economic impacts of automation. These measures can provide a buffer for displaced workers and help redistribute the gains from automation more equitably across society.

There is an opportunity to rethink the nature of work itself, exploring how automation can enhance human creativity and productivity rather than simply replacing human labor. This could involve the redesign of jobs to focus on tasks that leverage human strengths, such as emotional intelligence, creativity, and strategic thinking.

While automation poses significant challenges to the future of work, it also offers the potential for a more efficient and innovative economy. Navigating this transition successfully will require proactive measures to ensure that the benefits of automation are shared broadly, fostering an inclusive economy that values human well-being alongside technological progress.

While technology offers incredible opportunities for innovation and connection, it also presents significant challenges that must be navigated with care. The dual nature of digital life, as both a source of connection and isolation, underscores the need for a balanced approach to technology use. Similarly, the impacts of social media on self-esteem and the uncertainties surrounding automation and employment highlight the complexities of living in a technologically advanced society. By understanding these dynamics, we can better prepare for the future, ensuring that technology serves to enhance, rather than undermine, our collective well-being.

Part III: The Generation at the Heart

Chapter 6: A Portrait of a Generation

In this chapter, we look into the generational cohorts at the center of the current Fourth Turning, focusing on their defining characteristics, aspirations, anxieties, and the role of education in their lives. This exploration is critical for understanding the unique challenges and opportunities that define the era and for envisioning pathways toward a more hopeful future.

Defining the Generational Cohorts: Who Are They?

The current Fourth Turning primarily involves two generational cohorts: Millennials (born approximately between 1981 and 1996) and Generation Z (born approximately between 1997 and 2012). These groups are distinguished not only by their age but also by the unique social, economic, and technological landscapes that have shaped their upbringing and worldview.

Millennials came of age during the turn of the millennium, a time marked by rapid technological advancement and global interconnectedness. They were the first generation to grow up with the internet as a part of everyday life, which has influenced their approaches to communication, work, and social engagement. Economically, they entered adulthood during the Great Recession, which has had a lasting impact on their financial stability and outlook on the economic system.

Generation Z, on the other hand, has been shaped by the realities of a post-9/11 world, characterized by heightened awareness of global terrorism, climate change, and political polarization. They are true digital natives, having been exposed to the internet, social media, and mobile technology from a very young age. This exposure has affected their learning styles, social interactions, and expectations from life and work.

Values, Hopes, and Fears: What Matters to Them

Both Millennials and Generation Z are characterized by a set of values that reflects a departure from those of previous generations. They place a high emphasis on authenticity, social responsibility, and inclusivity. Environmental sustainability, social justice, and mental health are key concerns, driven by a deep-seated belief in the importance of making a positive impact on the world.

However, these values are often juxtaposed with their hopes and fears for the future. Many from these generations aspire to achieve traditional markers of success—stable careers, home ownership, and a better quality of life than their parents. Yet, they are also acutely aware of the barriers that stand in their way, including economic instability, the climate crisis, and the competitive job market.

The fears that haunt these cohorts are not unfounded; they stem from real challenges such as job automation, political unrest, and the escalating costs of living. These anxieties are further compounded by a pervasive sense of disillusionment with institutions perceived to have failed them—governments, financial systems, and even higher education.

The Role of Education: Shaping or Misshaping Futures?

Education has traditionally been seen as the pathway to success, but for many Millennials and Gen Zers, the reality has been starkly different. The promise of a college degree translating into a well-paying job and a secure future has been eroded by the student debt crisis and an oversaturated job market. This disillusionment is not merely financial; it also reflects a broader questioning of the value of conventional education systems in a rapidly changing world.

The role of education in shaping the futures of these generations is multifaceted. On one hand, it has equipped them with the skills and knowledge necessary to navigate the complexities of the 21st century. On the other, it has also been a source of significant stress and uncertainty, leaving many to question the return on their educational investments.

In response, there is a growing movement among these cohorts towards alternative forms of education and career preparation, including online learning, vocational training, and entrepreneurial ventures. These alternatives reflect a broader desire for education systems that are more adaptable, relevant, and aligned with their values and aspirations.

The generational cohorts at the heart of the current Fourth Turning are navigating a landscape marked by unprecedented challenges and opportunities. Understanding who they are, what matters to them, and how they perceive their role in the world is crucial for addressing the crises of our time. By recognizing the unique contributions and perspectives of Millennials and Generation Z, society can begin to forge pathways toward a future that honors their aspirations while addressing the systemic issues that threaten their prospects. This chapter is a testament to the resilience, creativity, and potential of these generations to shape a world that reflects their values and hopes for the future.

Part III: The Generation at the Heart

Chapter 7: Disconnected Communities

This chapter explores the profound shifts in the fabric of community life, examining the decline of traditional local communities, the emergence of virtual communities, and the implications of reduced civic engagement. These trends offer a lens through which to view the broader social and psychological challenges facing current generations, particularly as they navigate the complexities of the Fourth Turning.

The Erosion of Local Communities and Its Impacts

The erosion of local communities in recent decades is a multifaceted phenomenon, driven by economic globalization, urbanization, and technological advancements. This decline is characterized by a decrease in face-to-face interactions, dwindling participation in local organizations (such as clubs, churches, and civic groups), and a general sense of alienation from one's physical neighbors. The impacts of this erosion are profound, contributing to feelings of isolation, increased mental health challenges, and a diminished sense of belonging and security.

Local communities have traditionally served as the bedrock of social support, providing networks of care, shared values, and mutual aid. The weakening of these bonds has left many individuals struggling to find their place in the world, yearning for a sense of connection that modern life often fails to provide. This disconnection from local communal life has also led to a decline in social trust and a fraying of the social fabric that underpins cooperative action and mutual understanding.

The Rise of Virtual Communities: A New Form of Belonging?

In contrast to the decline of local communities, the digital age has seen the rise of virtual communities, facilitated by the internet and social media platforms. These online spaces offer new forms of connection and belonging, allowing individuals to engage with like-minded people across the globe. Virtual communities can provide a sense of identity and support, especially for those who feel marginalized or misunderstood in their physical environments.

However, the nature of these virtual connections is complex. While they offer unprecedented opportunities for engagement, they also raise questions about the depth and quality of these interactions. The anonymity and disembodiment of online communication can sometimes lead to superficial connections, exacerbating feelings of loneliness and alienation. Moreover, the echo chambers created by algorithm-driven content can reinforce existing prejudices and limit exposure to diverse perspectives, hindering the development of a truly inclusive sense of community.

The Decline of Civic Engagement and Its Consequences

Civic engagement, defined as individual and collective actions designed to identify and address issues of public concern, has also seen a notable decline. This trend, characterized by decreased participation in voting, public service, and community organizing, has significant implications for democracy and societal well-being. The withdrawal from civic life reflects a broader disillusionment with political institutions and a feeling of powerlessness among the population.

The consequences of reduced civic engagement are far-reaching. It undermines the capacity of communities to effect change, weakens democratic governance, and contributes to a sense of disempowerment and cynicism among citizens. Moreover, it diminishes the collective ability to tackle pressing challenges, such as economic inequality, climate change, and social justice issues, leaving societies more fragmented and less resilient in the face of adversity.

The disconnection from local communities, coupled with the ambiguous nature of virtual connections and the decline in civic engagement, poses significant challenges for societal cohesion and individual well-being. Rebuilding a sense of community in the modern world requires a multifaceted approach that acknowledges the value of both physical and virtual spaces for connection. It also demands a renewed commitment to civic participation as a means of empowering individuals and fostering a more engaged, inclusive, and resilient society. This chapter underscores the importance of community in navigating the uncertainties of the Fourth Turning, calling for innovative solutions to bridge divides and rebuild the communal bonds essential for a thriving society.

Part IV: Precursors to Disaster

Chapter 8: Historical Lessons and Modern Parallels

In this chapter, we explore the historical precursors to societal disasters, drawing parallels between past upheavals and the present-day challenges that signal we may be on the brink of a similar fate. By examining the French Revolution, the social movements of the 1960s, the Great Depression, and the 2008 financial crisis, we aim to extract lessons that can inform our understanding of the current moment and potentially guide us toward averting disaster.

Societal Upheaval: From the French Revolution to the 1960s

The French Revolution stands as a profound example of societal upheaval, driven by widespread discontent with inequality, economic distress, and a disconnect between the ruling classes and the general populace. The revolution's initial quest for liberty, equality, and fraternity eventually spiraled into a period of extreme violence and instability, illustrating the dangers inherent in ignoring the needs and grievances of the people.

Similarly, the social movements of the 1960s across the globe, marked by demands for civil rights, peace, and justice, reflect a period of significant societal tension and transformation. These movements were fueled by a younger generation disillusioned with the status quo and eager for change, showcasing the powerful role of youth in shaping the course of history.

Both periods teach us about the potential for societal change when collective dissatisfaction reaches a boiling point. They also highlight the importance of responsive governance and the need for societal structures that can adapt to and address the evolving needs of their populations.

Economic Disasters and Their Aftermath: The Great Depression and 2008 Financial Crisis

The Great Depression, a devastating global economic downturn, serves as a stark reminder of the impacts of economic mismanagement and the interconnectedness of global economies. The widespread hardship and unemployment of the era led to a profound loss of faith in economic and political institutions, setting the stage for significant social and political changes.

The 2008 financial crisis, similarly, exposed the vulnerabilities of the global financial system and the devastating consequences of unchecked speculation and financial deregulation. The aftermath of the crisis saw a significant increase in economic inequality and a resurgence of populist sentiment, as people around the world questioned the fairness and resilience of the existing economic order.

Both events underscore the critical importance of robust economic policies and regulations that prioritize the welfare of the broader population. They also illustrate how economic disasters can serve as catalysts for broader societal and political transformations.

The Warning Signs: What History Teaches Us About Today

The historical events discussed above offer valuable lessons for understanding the current era. The warning signs of societal upheaval and disaster often include growing economic inequality, widespread disillusionment with institutions, and a younger generation eager for change. Today, we see many of these same indicators, from the growing gap between the rich and the poor to the widespread distrust in governmental and financial institutions, alongside a highly mobilized and socially conscious youth.

These parallels suggest that we may be nearing a critical juncture, similar to those that preceded significant historical upheavals. The lessons of history teach us the importance of acknowledging and addressing the root causes of discontent before they escalate into full-blown crises. They remind us of the need for inclusive, equitable policies that address the needs of the most vulnerable and for flexible, responsive governance that can navigate the complexities of the modern world.

In recognizing these warning signs and understanding their historical precedents, we have the opportunity to chart a different course. By learning from the past, we can work towards creating a more stable, equitable, and resilient society that avoids the pitfalls of previous generations and builds a future that is inclusive and prosperous for all.

Chapter 9: The Politics of Discontent

This chapter looks into the complex dynamics of political discontent that have emerged as significant precursors to societal instability and conflict. By examining the processes of polarization and radicalization, the resurgence of populism and nationalism, and the consequences of neglecting the moderate majority, we aim to shed light on the political undercurrents that threaten to disrupt social cohesion and democratic governance.

Polarization and Radicalization: The Fuel of Conflict

The contemporary political landscape is increasingly characterized by deep ideological divides and an erosion of common ground. This polarization is not merely a difference in policy preferences but a fundamental disagreement on the nature of truth, justice, and the role of government. Social media and echo chambers exacerbate these divides, providing platforms that amplify extreme views and create fertile ground for radicalization.

Polarization fuels conflict by demonizing the "other" and eroding the sense of shared identity and purpose that binds societies together. Radical groups, on both ends of the political spectrum, exploit these divisions, pushing narratives that reject compromise and vilify opposition. The transition from ideological extremism to physical violence becomes a dangerous possibility when individuals or groups believe their actions are justified to protect their vision for society.

The Rise of Populism and Nationalism: A Response to Disillusionment

In response to widespread disillusionment with the status quo, many have turned to populist and nationalist movements that promise to restore national greatness, protect traditional values, and prioritize the needs of the "common people" over the elite. These movements often gain traction by tapping into real economic grievances, cultural fears, and a sense of lost identity, offering simple solutions to complex problems.

While the appeal of populism and nationalism can be understood as a reaction to perceived neglect by the political establishment, these movements also pose significant risks. They can undermine democratic norms, stoke xenophobia and discrimination, and destabilize international relations. The simplistic us-versus-them narrative promoted by many populist leaders fails to address the root causes of societal issues and can lead to policies that exacerbate division and inequality.

The Danger of Ignoring the Middle: The Forgotten Majority

One of the critical dangers in the current political climate is the marginalization of the moderate majority—those who occupy the center of the political spectrum and whose voices are often drowned out by more vocal and extreme factions. This "forgotten majority" is crucial for the functioning of democratic societies, as they play a key role in facilitating compromise, understanding, and progress.

Neglecting the needs and concerns of the middle can lead to a sense of disenfranchisement and apathy, weakening the social fabric and diminishing the collective capacity to address challenges. Furthermore, when moderate voices are sidelined, the political space becomes polarized, leaving little room for the nuanced dialogue and cooperation necessary to solve complex societal problems.

The politics of discontent, characterized by polarization, the rise of populism and nationalism, and the neglect of the moderate majority, presents a significant challenge to social cohesion and democratic governance. To navigate these turbulent waters, it is imperative to foster open dialogue, rebuild trust in institutions, and create inclusive policies that address the root causes of disillusionment. By doing so, societies can hope to bridge divides, strengthen democracy, and avert the kind of conflict and instability that have marred history.

Part V: Toward Renewal

Chapter 10: Redefining Success and Prosperity

In the face of mounting crises and a generational turning point, there emerges a pressing need to redefine our concepts of success and prosperity. This chapter explores the limitations of traditional metrics like GDP in capturing societal well-being, advocates for the consideration of a Universal Basic Income (UBI) as a tool for addressing economic disparities, and calls for a transformative approach to education that emphasizes lifelong learning and adaptability.

Beyond GDP: New Measures of Societal Health and Success

Gross Domestic Product (GDP) has long been the standard measure of a nation's economic success, but it fails to account for the distribution of wealth, environmental degradation, and the well-being of citizens. As we grapple with the complexities of the 21st century, it becomes imperative to adopt more holistic measures that reflect the true health of a society.

Alternative metrics, such as the Genuine Progress Indicator (GPI) and the Human Development Index (HDI), offer a broader perspective, incorporating factors like environmental health, education, and inequality. Moreover, the concept of Gross National Happiness (GNH), pioneered by Bhutan, emphasizes the importance of spiritual, physical, social, and environmental health in assessing national prosperity.

Adopting these or similar measures requires a paradigm shift in how we define and pursue success, urging policymakers to prioritize sustainability, equity, and well-being over mere economic growth. Such a shift could lead to more balanced and meaningful development, ensuring that progress benefits all members of society.

The Case for a Universal Basic Income

The idea of a Universal Basic Income (UBI)—a regular, unconditional payment to all citizens—has gained traction as a potential solution to economic insecurity, inequality, and the challenges posed by automation. UBI represents a radical rethinking of social welfare, proposing a safety net that could empower individuals to pursue education, entrepreneurship, or other interests without the immediate pressure of financial survival.

Critics of UBI argue about its feasibility and potential to discourage work, yet trials and studies in various countries have shown promising outcomes, including reductions in poverty, improvements in health and education, and increased entrepreneurship. By providing a foundational level of financial security, UBI could foster a society where success is not solely defined by employment or wealth but by the ability to lead fulfilling and secure lives.

Education Reimagined: Lifelong Learning and Adaptability

The rapidly changing economic landscape, marked by technological advancement and shifting job markets, calls for an education system that prioritizes lifelong learning and adaptability over rote memorization and narrow specialization. The future of work requires a workforce that is flexible, creative, and capable of continuous learning.

Redefining education involves expanding access to diverse learning opportunities at all stages of life, including vocational training, digital literacy programs, and interdisciplinary studies. It also means recognizing and valuing informal and experiential learning alongside traditional academic achievements.

By fostering a culture of continuous growth and adaptability, we can prepare individuals not only to navigate the challenges of the future workforce but also to thrive in a world where change is the only constant. Such an approach to education underpins a broader vision of success and prosperity, one that values personal fulfillment, community engagement, and the ability to adapt to an ever-evolving world.

Redefining success and prosperity for the 21st century involves a holistic approach that considers economic, social, and environmental well-being. By moving beyond GDP, exploring the potential of universal basic income, and reimagining education, we can lay the groundwork for a society that values well-being and resilience over mere economic growth. This chapter outlines a path toward renewal, where success is measured not by wealth or status but by the health, happiness, and adaptability of individuals and communities. In facing the challenges of the Fourth Turning, such a redefinition is not just desirable but essential for building a more equitable and sustainable future.

Part V: Toward Renewal

Chapter 11: Building Resilient Communities

In an era defined by profound societal shifts and challenges, the restoration and strengthening of community resilience stand as pivotal endeavors. This chapter looks into the critical role of grassroots movements and local solutions in fostering resilient communities, explores the importance of social capital in rebuilding trust and engagement, and considers the potential of technology to enhance human connections rather than supplant them.

Grassroots Movements and Local Solutions

The foundation of resilient communities often lies in the power and efficacy of grassroots movements and local initiatives. These movements harness the collective energy, knowledge, and resources of community members to address local challenges, from environmental sustainability and economic development to social justice and healthcare.

Grassroots movements embody the principle of subsidiarity, which posits that decisions should be made as close as possible to the level of impact. This approach ensures that solutions are tailored to the unique needs and contexts of each community, fostering a sense of ownership and commitment among its members. Local solutions derived from grassroots efforts are often more sustainable and effective, as they are built on a deep understanding of the community's dynamics and challenges.

Case studies of successful grassroots initiatives, such as community-led urban gardens in food deserts or local renewable energy cooperatives, illustrate the potential of localized efforts to create significant, lasting impacts. These examples serve as blueprints for other communities seeking to enhance their resilience through collective action and innovation.

The Power of Social Capital: Rebuilding Trust and Engagement

Social capital, defined as the networks of relationships among people who live and work in a particular society, enabling that society to function effectively, is a critical asset for community resilience. It encompasses elements of trust, reciprocity, and shared norms that facilitate cooperation and support among community members.

In times of crisis or transition, such as those characteristic of a Fourth Turning, the importance of social capital becomes even more pronounced. Rebuilding trust and engagement within communities can provide the social cohesion necessary to navigate challenges, adapt to changes, and implement collective solutions.

Efforts to strengthen social capital can include fostering inclusive public spaces, encouraging civic participation, and promoting community events and initiatives that bring people together. Such efforts not only enhance the fabric of community life but also build the trust and networks that can mobilize resources and support in times of need.

Technology as a Tool for Good: Enhancing Rather Than Replacing Human Connections

While technology has often been critiqued for its role in eroding face-to-face interactions and contributing to social isolation, it also holds the potential to strengthen community ties and enhance resilience. The key lies in leveraging technology as a tool for good—enhancing rather than replacing human connections.

Digital platforms can facilitate the sharing of information, resources, and support across community networks, breaking down barriers of distance and time. Social media, when used constructively, can amplify local initiatives, engage broader audiences, and foster a sense of community solidarity. Moreover, technology can enhance accessibility to education, healthcare, and economic opportunities, particularly for marginalized or remote populations.

The challenge and opportunity lie in designing and utilizing technology in ways that foster genuine connection, inclusivity, and support. This involves creating digital spaces that encourage meaningful interactions, protect privacy, and promote positive community engagement.

Building resilient communities in the context of the Fourth Turning requires a multifaceted approach that embraces grassroots movements, strengthens social capital, and harnesses technology for the greater good. By focusing on local solutions, rebuilding trust and engagement, and leveraging digital tools to enhance human connections, communities can navigate the challenges of this era with greater cohesion, adaptability, and strength. This chapter outlines a roadmap for cultivating community resilience, emphasizing the power of collective action, shared values, and innovative solutions to build a more hopeful and sustainable future.

Epilogue: The Path Forward

As we conclude our exploration of the Fourth Turning, its impact on society, and the potential pathways toward renewal, it's essential to reflect on the lessons learned and chart a course for the future. This epilogue serves as both a summation of our journey and a clarion call to action for individuals and communities across generational divides.

Lessons Learned and the Road Ahead

The journey through the Fourth Turning reveals a tapestry of challenges and opportunities. We've seen how historical cycles inform our understanding of current societal upheavals and how economic, social, and technological forces shape the landscape of our lives. From the disillusionment faced by younger generations to the erosion of community and the divisive nature of politics, the challenges are formidable. Yet, within these challenges lie the seeds of transformation.

One of the most critical lessons is the importance of adaptability and resilience—qualities that must be cultivated not just individually but within the very fabric of our communities and institutions. The path forward requires a reimagining of success, prosperity, and the nature of work and education. It demands a shift towards inclusivity, sustainability, and well-being as central tenets of societal progress.

Another lesson is the power of collective action and grassroots movements in driving change. The rebuilding of social capital and trust, essential for cohesive communities, begins with engagement at the local level. Technology, too, plays a pivotal role, offering unprecedented opportunities for connection and collaboration, even as we navigate its challenges and potential to isolate.

As we look to the future, the road ahead is both uncertain and promising. The choices we make today—individually and collectively—will determine the trajectory of the coming years and decades. This moment in history, the Fourth Turning, is not just a crisis but an opportunity to reshape our world, reflecting the values of equity, sustainability, and shared prosperity.

A Call to Action for All Generations

This moment demands action from us all, irrespective of generational cohort. To the older generations, there is a responsibility to mentor, support, and pass on the wisdom that comes with experience. There is a wealth of knowledge to be shared, not as a prescriptive path forward but as a guiding light, illuminating the possibilities that lie ahead.

To the younger generations, the call to action is to engage, innovate, and lead the charge toward change. Armed with the insights of the past and the technologies of the present, there is an opportunity to redefine the future, to build a world that aligns more closely with the ideals of inclusivity, sustainability, and shared humanity.

For all generations, the call is to listen, to collaborate, and to build bridges. The challenges we face are interconnected and complex, requiring a united effort that transcends generational, political, and cultural divides. It's a call to foster community, to engage in civic life, and to participate in the ongoing project of society-building.

The Fourth Turning is not an end but a beginning, a chance to reflect on where we've been and to decide where we want to go. The path forward is fraught with challenges, but it is also ripe with opportunity. By learning from the past, engaging with the present, and planning for the future, we can navigate the tumult of this era and emerge into a period of renewal and hope.

This epilogue, and the book as a whole, is an invitation to all who envision a better future. It's a reminder that the power to shape the next chapter of our story lies in our hands. Together, let us embark on the path forward, guided by the lessons of the Fourth Turning and motivated by the promise of a brighter tomorrow.

Not Built For This

Julian Del Bel

Table of Contents:

Part I. Introduction
  1. Setting the Stage: From Hunter-Gatherers to Post-Industrial Civilization
  2. The Evolutionary Legacy: How Our Past Shapes Our Present

Part II. The Post-Industrial Shift: A Paradigm in Flux
  3. Defining the Post-Industrial Era
  4. The Acceleration of Technological Advancement
  5. Shifting Societal Structures: Urbanization and Globalization

Part III. The Psychological Landscape of Post-Industrialism
  6. Disconnect from Nature: Consequences of Urbanization
  7. Digital Dilemmas: The Impact of Technology on Human Interaction
  8. Consumer Culture: Materialism and Its Psychological Ramifications

Part IV. Evolutionary Mismatch: When Our Biology Clashes with Modernity
  9. From Movement to Sedentarism: The Toll of Desk Jobs and Sedentary Lifestyles
  10. Dietary Disparity: Evolutionary Mismatch in Modern Diets
  11. Sleep Deprivation and Circadian Disruptions: Consequences of 24/7 Connectivity

Part V. Psychosocial Effects of Post-Industrialism
  12. Social Fragmentation: Loneliness and Isolation in the Digital Age
  13. Mental Health Epidemic: Anxiety, Depression, and the Modern Psyche

14. Existential Crises: Navigating Meaning and Purpose in a Consumerist Society

Part VI. Resilience and Adaptation: Coping Mechanisms in a Post-Industrial World
15. Reconnecting with Nature: The Healing Power of Green Spaces
16. Digital Detox: Strategies for Reclaiming Balance in the Digital Age
17. Cultivating Community: Building Resilient Social Networks in Urban Environments

VII. Towards a Harmonious Future: Reconciling Humanity's Past with its Present
18. Sustainable Living: Balancing Technological Progress with Environmental Stewardship
19. Human-Centric Design: Creating Spaces and Systems that Nurture Well-Being
20. Mindful Consumption: Fostering Consciousness in a Culture of Excess

Part VIII. Conclusion
21. Reflections on the Journey: Insights Gained from Exploring Humanity's Psyche
22. Charting the Course Forward: Opportunities for Collective Growth and Evolution
23. Embracing the Complexity: Honoring the Interplay of Human Nature and Post-Industrial Progress

Part I. Introduction

Chapter 1: Setting the Stage: From Hunter-Gatherers to Post-Industrial Civilization

In the beginning, there was the wilderness. Endless stretches of untamed land, teeming with life and possibility. This was the domain of our ancestors, the hunter-gatherers who roamed the earth tens of thousands of years ago. Picture them, if you will, nomads of the ancient world, their sinewy forms blending seamlessly with the natural landscape as they pursued sustenance and survival.

These were humans in their rawest form, intimately attuned to the rhythms of nature. Every dawn brought with it the promise of a new hunt, a fresh forage, a primal dance of life and death played out on the stage of the wilderness. They knew the land like the lines on their weathered palms, reading the signs and signals of the earth with a wisdom born of necessity. But as the millennia passed, something shifted in the fabric of human existence. The fires of industry began to burn, fueled by the discovery of agriculture and the rise of settled civilizations. No longer did humanity wander freely across the plains; instead, we built cities and kingdoms, carving our mark upon the land with plowshares and swords.

With the advent of the industrial revolution, the pace of change quickened, propelling us headlong into a new era of progress and innovation. Machines replaced muscle, steam and steel supplanted sinew and bone, and the landscape of our world was forever altered. Where once there had been vast wilderness, now there were factories belching smoke into the sky, and sprawling cities pulsating with the frenetic energy of human endeavor.

And so we find ourselves in the present day, heirs to a legacy forged in the crucible of history. Our journey from hunter-gatherers to post-industrial citizens has been one of unparalleled transformation, marked by triumph and tragedy, innovation and destruction. We stand at the precipice of a new frontier, poised on the brink of a future that is both wondrous and uncertain. But amidst the dizzying whirl of progress, we must not forget the lessons of our past. For in the wilderness of our origins lie the roots of our humanity, tangled and intertwined with the very fabric of existence. As we navigate the uncharted terrain of the post-industrial world, let us heed the wisdom of our ancestors and tread lightly upon the earth.

Chapter 2: The Evolutionary Legacy: How Our Past Shapes Our Present

To truly understand the intricacies of our modern existence, we must first delve into the depths of our evolutionary heritage. For woven into the very fabric of our being are the echoes of our ancestors, whispering secrets of survival and adaptation that continue to shape our lives today.

At the heart of our evolutionary legacy lies the concept of natural selection, the driving force behind the gradual transformation of our species over countless generations. Through the process of adaptation, those individuals best suited to their environment were more likely to survive and reproduce, passing on their advantageous traits to future generations. In the primordial crucible of prehistory, our ancestors faced a myriad of challenges, from harsh climates to fierce predators. But it was their ability to adapt and innovate that allowed them to thrive in even the most unforgiving of environments. From the development of tools and fire to the emergence of complex social structures, each step forward marked a triumph of ingenuity over adversity.

One of the defining features of our evolutionary journey is our capacity for cooperation and social bonding. For millions of years, humans have lived in tight-knit groups, relying on one another for protection, sustenance, and companionship. This innate drive towards social cohesion has left an indelible mark on our psychology, shaping everything from our moral values to our patterns of communication. But perhaps the most profound legacy of our evolutionary past is our deep-seated connection to the natural world. For countless generations, our ancestors lived in intimate harmony with the rhythms of the earth, drawing sustenance from its bounty and finding solace in its beauty. Even as we have built towering skyscrapers and sprawling cities, we remain inexorably linked to the land that birthed us. Yet, for all our progress and innovation, we must not forget that we are still creatures of flesh and blood, shaped by millions of years of evolution. Our bodies bear the scars of our ancient past, from the curvature of our spines to the structure of our brains. And though we may have conquered mountains and crossed oceans, we are still bound by the same fundamental laws of nature that govern all life on earth.

As we navigate the complexities of the modern world, let us never lose sight of the profound legacy that has brought us to this point. For in understanding where we come from, we gain insight into who we are and where we are headed. And though the challenges we face may be daunting, we can take comfort in the knowledge that we carry with us the resilience and adaptability of countless generations who have come before.

Part II. The Post-Industrial Shift: A Paradigm in Flux

Chapter 3: Defining the Post-Industrial Era

The transition from an industrial to a post-industrial society marks a pivotal moment in human history, a seismic shift in the very foundations of our civilization. But what exactly defines this enigmatic era, and how does it differ from the industrial age that preceded it?

At its core, the post-industrial era is characterized by a fundamental reorientation of economic, social, and technological paradigms. Where once the driving force of progress was the manufacturing of goods, now it is the creation and exchange of information that takes center stage. Gone are the smokestacks and assembly lines of the industrial age, replaced by the sleek surfaces of digital interfaces and the ethereal networks of cyberspace.

Central to the post-industrial landscape is the rise of the knowledge economy, in which value is increasingly derived from the production and dissemination of knowledge and information. This shift has profound implications for the nature of work and employment, as traditional blue-collar jobs are supplanted by roles in fields such as technology, finance, and creative industries.

But the post-industrial era is not simply defined by changes in economic structure; it also encompasses profound transformations in social organization and cultural values. As societies become increasingly urbanized and interconnected, traditional hierarchies and modes of governance are challenged by new forms of social organization and collective action.

Technological innovation lies at the heart of the post-industrial revolution, driving change at an unprecedented pace and scale. From the advent of the internet to the proliferation of smartphones and social media, technology has reshaped the very fabric of human interaction, blurring the boundaries between virtual and physical worlds. Yet, for all its promise and potential, the post-industrial era is not without its challenges and contradictions. The same forces of globalization and digitization that have fueled economic growth and innovation have also given rise to widening inequalities and social fragmentation. As wealth becomes increasingly concentrated in the hands of a privileged few, vast swaths of society are left behind, trapped in a cycle of economic insecurity and marginalization.

The relentless march of technological progress brings with it a host of ethical dilemmas and existential questions. From concerns about privacy and surveillance to debates over the impact of automation on employment, the post-industrial era forces us to confront the very essence of what it means to be human in an age of machines. In defining the post-industrial era, we are confronted with a complex and multifaceted phenomenon, one that defies easy categorization or understanding. Yet, as we grapple with the challenges and opportunities of this brave new world, one thing is clear: the post-industrial era represents a turning point in human history, a moment of reckoning and renewal as we chart a course towards an uncertain future.

Chapter 4: The Acceleration of Technological Advancement

In the annals of human history, few phenomena have had as profound an impact on society as the relentless march of technological advancement. From the discovery of fire to the invention of the wheel, from the printing press to the steam engine, each technological innovation has reshaped the contours of human civilization, propelling us ever forward into the unknown. But never before has the pace of technological progress been so rapid, so relentless, as it is in the present day. We live in an age of unprecedented innovation, where breakthroughs in science and technology occur with dizzying frequency, transforming the world around us in ways both profound and unpredictable.

Central to this acceleration of technological advancement is the phenomenon known as Moore's Law, which states that the number of transistors on a microchip doubles approximately every two years, leading to exponential increases in computing power. This exponential growth has fueled a cascade of innovation across a wide range of fields, from artificial intelligence and machine learning to biotechnology and nanotechnology.

The implications of this technological revolution are staggering, touching every aspect of human life and society. In the realm of communication, the advent of the internet and mobile technology has ushered in an era of instant connectivity, allowing people to communicate and collaborate across vast distances with unprecedented ease.

In the field of medicine, advances in genomics and personalized medicine hold the promise of revolutionizing healthcare, offering tailored treatments and therapies based on an individual's unique genetic makeup. From the development of targeted cancer therapies to the creation of artificial organs through 3D printing, the possibilities are as limitless as they are awe-inspiring. Yet, for all its transformative potential, the acceleration of technological advancement also raises profound ethical and existential questions. As artificial intelligence grows ever more sophisticated, what will become of the human workforce? Will automation lead to widespread unemployment, or will it free us from the drudgery of repetitive tasks, allowing us to pursue more meaningful and creative pursuits?

As we entrust more and more of our lives to technology, what safeguards are in place to protect our privacy and security? From the proliferation of surveillance technologies to the specter of cyberwarfare, the dangers posed by our increasing reliance on digital infrastructure are manifold and complex.

In navigating the brave new world of accelerated technological advancement, we are confronted with a dizzying array of possibilities and pitfalls. Yet, as we stand on the cusp of this technological frontier, one thing is certain: the future belongs to those who dare to dream, to innovate, and to harness the power of technology for the greater good of humanity.

Part III. The Psychological Landscape of Post-Industrialism

Chapter 5: Shifting Societal Structures: Urbanization and Globalization

As humanity hurtles forward into the 21st century, our world is undergoing a profound transformation, reshaping the very fabric of society as we know it. At the heart of this transformation lie two interconnected phenomena: urbanization and globalization. Together, these forces are driving a seismic shift in societal structures, redefining the way we live, work, and interact with one another.

Urbanization, the process by which people migrate from rural areas to cities, has been accelerating at an unprecedented pace in recent decades. Today, more than half of the world's population resides in urban areas, a trend that shows no signs of slowing down. From the towering skyscrapers of megacities like Tokyo and New York to the sprawling slums of Mumbai and Lagos, cities have become the epicenters of human civilization, pulsating with the energy of millions of souls striving to carve out a place for themselves in the modern world. But urbanization is not just about the physical concentration of people; it also entails profound changes in social and cultural dynamics. In cities, people from diverse backgrounds and walks of life come together, forging new identities and communities in the melting pot of urban life. From the rise of multiculturalism and cosmopolitanism to the emergence of vibrant subcultures and countercultures, cities are incubators of creativity and innovation, pushing the boundaries of what is possible.

Alongside the promise of opportunity and progress, urbanization also brings with it a host of challenges and inequalities. In many cities, rapid population growth has outstripped infrastructure and services, leading to overcrowding, pollution, and social unrest. Moreover, as wealth becomes increasingly concentrated in urban centers, marginalized communities are often left behind, trapped in cycles of poverty and deprivation.

Globalization, meanwhile, refers to the interconnectedness and interdependence of economies, cultures, and societies on a global scale. Enabled by advances in transportation and communication technology, globalization has transformed the world into a global village, where goods, ideas, and people flow freely across borders, transcending traditional barriers of time and space.

From the rise of multinational corporations and supply chains to the spread of cultural exchange and intercultural dialogue, globalization has created a web of connections that spans the globe. Yet, it has also led to a homogenization of culture and the erosion of local traditions and identities, as global forces exert their influence on even the most remote corners of the earth.

In navigating the complex terrain of urbanization and globalization, we are confronted with a dizzying array of opportunities and challenges. From the need to create sustainable and inclusive cities to the imperative of fostering cross-cultural understanding and cooperation, the task ahead is daunting but not insurmountable. As we stand on the threshold of a new era in human history, let us embrace the promise of urbanization and globalization, harnessing their transformative power to build a more equitable, resilient, and interconnected world for generations to come.

Chapter 6: Disconnect from Nature: Consequences of Urbanization

Urbanization, the process of population concentration in cities, has fundamentally reshaped the human experience, altering our relationship with the natural world in profound ways. As more and more people migrate from rural areas to urban centers, our connection to the natural environment is increasingly attenuated, leading to a host of consequences for both individuals and society as a whole.

One of the most immediate consequences of urbanization is the loss of access to green spaces and natural environments. In densely populated cities, green spaces are often scarce, relegated to small parks or manicured gardens amidst a sea of concrete and steel. This lack of access to nature can have detrimental effects on physical and mental well-being, depriving city dwellers of the restorative benefits of natural environments.

Studies have shown that exposure to green spaces can reduce stress, improve mood, and enhance cognitive function. Yet, for many urban residents, access to nature is limited, leading to higher rates of anxiety, depression, and other mental health disorders. This disconnect from nature can also contribute to a sense of alienation and disconnection from the world around us, leading to feelings of loneliness and isolation.

The loss of green spaces and natural habitats in urban areas has negative implications for biodiversity and ecological sustainability. As cities expand and encroach upon natural habitats, wildlife populations are displaced or destroyed, leading to declines in species diversity and ecosystem health. This loss of biodiversity can have far-reaching consequences, impacting everything from ecosystem stability to human livelihoods and food security. Urbanization often results in increased pollution and environmental degradation, further exacerbating the disconnect from nature. Air and water pollution, noise pollution, and light pollution are all common features of urban environments, posing significant threats to human health and well-being. Moreover, the loss of natural habitats and green spaces can contribute to the urban heat island effect, exacerbating the impacts of climate change and increasing the risk of heat-related illnesses and deaths.

Dealing through the consequences of urbanization, it is clear that reconnecting with nature is essential for human health, well-being, and ecological sustainability. Efforts to green urban environments, expand access to parks and natural areas, and promote sustainable development practices are critical steps towards fostering a more harmonious relationship between cities and the natural world. By prioritizing the preservation and restoration of green spaces and natural habitats, we can create healthier, happier, and more resilient cities for generations to come.

Chapter 7: Digital Dilemmas: The Impact of Technology on Human Interaction

Technology has become an omnipresent force in our lives, transforming the way we communicate, connect, and interact with one another. From smartphones and social media to video conferencing and virtual reality, the digital landscape offers unprecedented opportunities for connection and collaboration. Yet, amidst the promise of instant communication and global connectivity, there lurks a shadow side, as the relentless march of technology threatens to erode the very fabric of human interaction.

One of the most pressing dilemmas posed by digital technology is the erosion of face-to-face communication and interpersonal relationships. In an era dominated by screens and devices, many of us find ourselves increasingly reliant on digital communication platforms to stay connected with friends, family, and colleagues. While these platforms offer convenience and efficiency, they also lack the nuance and depth of face-to-face interaction, leading to a sense of disconnection and isolation. The rise of social media has fundamentally altered the nature of human interaction, blurring the boundaries between public and private spheres and reshaping our sense of identity and self-worth. On social media platforms, we curate carefully crafted personas, projecting idealized versions of ourselves to the world while concealing our vulnerabilities and insecurities. This culture of comparison and competition can lead to feelings of inadequacy and low self-esteem, as we constantly measure ourselves against unrealistic standards of perfection.

The ubiquity of digital technology has given rise to new forms of addiction and compulsive behavior, as we become increasingly tethered to our devices and platforms. From the dopamine hit of receiving likes and notifications to the endless scroll of news feeds and timelines, the digital landscape is designed to keep us hooked, feeding our insatiable appetite for validation and stimulation.

But perhaps the most insidious impact of digital technology on human interaction is its role in perpetuating echo chambers and filter bubbles, exacerbating polarization and ideological extremism. On social media platforms and news websites, algorithms prioritize content that aligns with our existing beliefs and preferences, creating echo chambers where dissenting voices are silenced and opposing viewpoints are demonized. This narrowing of perspective can fuel tribalism and divisiveness, undermining the very foundations of civil discourse and democratic society.

Facing the impact of digital technology on human interaction, it is clear that we must strike a delicate balance between the benefits and pitfalls of technological advancement. While digital communication platforms offer unparalleled opportunities for connection and collaboration, they also pose significant risks to our mental health, social cohesion, and democratic values. By fostering a critical awareness of the ways in which technology shapes our lives and relationships, we can harness its transformative potential while mitigating its harmful effects, creating a more inclusive, equitable, and compassionate digital future.

Chapter 8: Consumer Culture: Materialism and Its Psychological Ramifications

Consumer culture reigns supreme, shaping the way we define ourselves, relate to others, and navigate the world around us. At its core, consumer culture is driven by the relentless pursuit of material possessions and status symbols, as we seek to fill the void within ourselves with external markers of success and identity. Yet, beneath the glossy veneer of consumerism lies a darker reality, as the relentless pursuit of material wealth and possessions exacts a heavy toll on our psychological well-being and sense of fulfillment.

One of the most detrimental effects of consumer culture is its promotion of materialism, the belief that happiness and fulfillment can be found through the acquisition of material possessions. In a consumer-driven society, we are bombarded with messages that equate wealth and possessions with happiness and success, leading many of us to define ourselves and our worth in terms of what we own rather than who we are.

This obsession with material wealth and possessions can lead to a host of negative psychological outcomes, including feelings of emptiness, inadequacy, and discontent. Research has shown that materialistic individuals are more likely to experience higher levels of stress, anxiety, and depression, as they constantly strive to keep up with the unrealistic standards set by consumer culture.

The pursuit of material wealth and possessions can also have detrimental effects on our relationships and social connections. In a society that values material success above all else, interpersonal relationships can become commodified, as we judge others based on their possessions and social status rather than their intrinsic worth as human beings. This can lead to feelings of alienation and loneliness, as genuine connection and intimacy are sacrificed on the altar of materialism.

The relentless pursuit of material possessions can have devastating consequences for the environment and future generations. In our quest for more, faster, and better, we consume natural resources at an unsustainable rate, leading to environmental degradation, pollution, and climate change. This not only threatens the health and well-being of present and future generations but also perpetuates a cycle of consumption and destruction that is ultimately unsustainable.

Witnessing the psychological ramifications of consumer culture, it is clear that we must challenge the pervasive notion that happiness and fulfillment can be found through the acquisition of material possessions. Instead, we must cultivate a culture of gratitude, mindfulness, and meaningful connection, recognizing that true happiness lies not in what we own but in who we are and how we relate to the world around us. By prioritizing experiences over possessions, relationships over status, and sustainability over consumption, we can create a more equitable, compassionate, and sustainable society for all.

Part IV. Evolutionary Mismatch: When Our Biology Clashes with Modernity

Chapter 9: From Movement to Sedentarism: The Toll of Desk Jobs and Sedentary Lifestyles

Technological advancements and shifts in economic structure have led to a profound transformation in the way we work, live, and move our bodies. Once, our ancestors lived lives characterized by constant movement and physical exertion, as they hunted, gathered, and traversed vast distances in search of sustenance and shelter. Today, however, many of us find ourselves trapped in a sedentary lifestyle, tethered to desks and screens for the majority of our waking hours. This shift from movement to sedentarism has far-reaching consequences for our physical health, mental well-being, and overall quality of life.

At the heart of the rise in sedentary lifestyles is the prevalence of desk jobs and occupations that require long hours of sitting and minimal physical activity. In offices and cubicles around the world, workers spend the bulk of their days hunched over computers, typing away at keyboards and staring at screens for hours on end. This prolonged sitting not only leads to physical discomfort and musculoskeletal issues but also has serious implications for our long-term health and well-being.

Research has shown that sedentary behavior is associated with a host of negative health outcomes, including obesity, cardiovascular disease, type 2 diabetes, and even certain types of cancer. Sitting for extended periods of time can lead to decreased metabolic rate, poor circulation, and increased risk of blood clots, all of which contribute to the development of chronic health conditions. Moreover, sedentary behavior is also linked to mental health issues such as depression and anxiety, as well as decreased cognitive function and productivity.

The rise in sedentary lifestyles has broader societal implications, as it contributes to rising healthcare costs, decreased productivity, and decreased quality of life. As more and more people spend their days sitting at desks and screens, rates of chronic diseases and health conditions related to sedentary behavior continue to rise, placing an increasing burden on healthcare systems and economies around the world.

Through realizing the toll of desk jobs and sedentary lifestyles, it is clear that we must prioritize movement and physical activity in our daily lives. By incorporating regular exercise, breaks from sitting, and ergonomic adjustments into our work routines, we can mitigate the negative effects of sedentary behavior and promote overall health and well-being. Moreover, employers and policymakers must take action to create work environments that encourage movement and physical activity, whether through workplace wellness programs, flexible work arrangements, or incentives for active commuting. By prioritizing movement and physical activity, we can reclaim our health, vitality, and zest for life in an increasingly sedentary world.

Chapter 10: Dietary Disparity: Evolutionary Mismatch in Modern Diets

Throughout the course of human evolution, our dietary habits have undergone significant changes, shaped by shifts in environment, culture, and technology. For millions of years, our ancestors subsisted on a diet of wild plants, lean meats, and seasonal fruits, adapted to the rhythms of the natural world. Yet, in the blink of an eye, the agricultural revolution transformed the way we eat, ushering in an era of abundance and dietary diversity.

Today, however, our modern diets bear little resemblance to those of our ancestors, as we find ourselves confronted with a dizzying array of processed foods, refined sugars, and artificial additives. This dietary disparity, characterized by a mismatch between our evolutionary past and our present-day food environment, has far-reaching implications for our health, well-being, and longevity.
At the heart of the dietary disparity lies the phenomenon of the "Western diet," characterized by high levels of processed foods, refined sugars, unhealthy fats, and animal products. This diet, which

is high in calories and low in essential nutrients, has been linked to a host of chronic health conditions, including obesity, type 2 diabetes, heart disease, and certain types of cancer. Moreover, the Western diet is also associated with poor gut health, inflammation, and dysregulation of metabolic processes, further increasing the risk of chronic disease.

One of the primary drivers of the dietary disparity is the rise of industrial agriculture and food processing, which has led to the mass production and distribution of cheap, calorie-dense foods that are high in sugar, salt, and unhealthy fats. These highly processed foods, which are often engineered to be hyper-palatable and addictive, contribute to overeating, weight gain, and metabolic dysfunction, driving rates of obesity and related health conditions to unprecedented levels.

The dietary disparity is compounded by socioeconomic factors, as access to healthy, nutritious foods is often limited by income, education, and geographic location. In many communities, particularly those in urban food deserts and rural areas, fresh fruits, vegetables, and whole grains are prohibitively expensive or simply unavailable, leading to reliance on cheap, processed foods that are high in calories and low in nutrients.

In coming to terms with the dietary disparity, it is clear that we must prioritize access to healthy, nutritious foods for all members of society. By promoting policies that support sustainable agriculture, local food systems, and equitable access to fresh, whole foods, we can create environments that make healthy eating the easy and affordable choice for everyone. Moreover, by raising awareness of the dangers of the Western diet and empowering individuals to make informed dietary choices, we can reverse the tide of chronic disease and create a healthier, more resilient future for generations to come.

Chapter 11: Sleep Deprivation and Circadian Disruptions: Consequences of 24/7 Connectivity

In today's hyper-connected world, the boundaries between day and night, work and leisure, have become increasingly blurred, as we find ourselves immersed in a 24/7 cycle of connectivity and productivity. Yet, amidst the constant buzz of notifications and the glow of screens, a silent epidemic rages, one that threatens our health, well-being, and quality of life: sleep deprivation and circadian disruptions.

At the heart of the issue lies our increasing reliance on technology and artificial light, which has disrupted the natural rhythms of our circadian clock, the internal biological clock that regulates our sleep-wake cycle. From smartphones and tablets to laptops and televisions, the devices that keep us connected to the world around us emit blue light, a type of light that suppresses the production of melatonin, the hormone that regulates sleep. Our 24/7 culture of connectivity has led to a normalization of sleep deprivation, as we sacrifice precious hours of rest in pursuit of productivity and achievement. Whether it's burning the midnight oil to meet a deadline or scrolling through social media feeds into the wee hours of the morning, many of us are chronically sleep-deprived, unaware of the toll that our nocturnal habits are taking on our health and well-being.

The consequences of sleep deprivation and circadian disruptions are far-reaching, affecting nearly every aspect of our physical and mental health. In the short term, sleep deprivation can lead to decreased cognitive function, impaired memory and concentration, and increased irritability and moodiness. Over time, chronic sleep deprivation is associated with a host of serious health conditions, including obesity, type 2 diabetes, heart disease, and even certain types of cancer.

Sleep deprivation has profound implications for mental health, increasing the risk of anxiety, depression, and other mood disorders. Studies have shown that sleep disturbances are closely linked to disruptions in brain function and neurotransmitter activity, leading to alterations in mood regulation and emotional processing.

Sleep deprivation and circadian disruptions can also have negative effects on immune function, increasing susceptibility to illness and infection. During sleep, the body repairs and replenishes itself, strengthening the immune system and fortifying defenses against pathogens. Yet, when sleep is disrupted or inadequate, the body's ability to fight off infections is compromised, leaving us vulnerable to illness and disease.

In facing the consequences of 24/7 connectivity on sleep and circadian rhythms, it is clear that we must prioritize rest and relaxation as essential components of a healthy lifestyle. By adopting healthy sleep habits, such as maintaining a consistent sleep schedule, creating a relaxing bedtime routine, and limiting exposure to screens and artificial light before bed, we can reclaim our natural rhythms and restore balance to our lives. Moreover, by raising awareness of the importance of sleep and advocating for policies that support work-life balance and employee well-being, we can create environments that prioritize health and happiness over productivity at any cost.

Part V. Psychosocial Effects of Post-Industrialism

Chapter 12: Social Fragmentation: Loneliness and Isolation in the Digital Age

In the digital age, we are more connected than ever before, able to communicate with anyone, anywhere, at any time with the tap of a screen. Yet, paradoxically, many of us find ourselves feeling lonelier and more isolated than ever before. This phenomenon of social fragmentation, characterized by a sense of disconnection and alienation despite the prevalence of digital communication, is a growing concern in our increasingly interconnected world.

At the heart of social fragmentation lies the erosion of meaningful social connections and the breakdown of community ties. In the digital age, social interactions have become increasingly mediated by screens and devices, leading to a superficiality and shallowness in our relationships. Instead of engaging in face-to-face conversations and shared experiences, we often find ourselves scrolling through social media feeds, passively consuming content without truly connecting with others. The rise of social media has led to the proliferation of curated personas and idealized lifestyles, creating a culture of comparison and competition that exacerbates feelings of inadequacy and loneliness. As we scroll through carefully curated feeds filled with images of smiling faces and glamorous lifestyles, we can't help but compare our own lives to the polished perfection presented online, leading to feelings of isolation and self-doubt.

The prevalence of digital communication has led to a decline in in-person social interactions and community engagement. Instead of gathering in person for social events and activities, many of us rely on virtual interactions to fulfill our social needs, leading to a sense of disconnection from the world around us. This lack of meaningful social engagement can contribute to feelings of loneliness and isolation, as we struggle to find genuine connections in a world dominated by screens and devices.

The consequences of social fragmentation are profound and far-reaching, affecting both our physical and mental health. Studies have shown that chronic loneliness is associated with increased risk of a wide range of health problems, including cardiovascular disease, depression, anxiety, and even premature death. Moreover, loneliness can also have negative effects on cognitive function and immune function, further compromising overall health and well-being.

In confronting the challenge of social fragmentation in the digital age, it is clear that we must prioritize meaningful social connections and community engagement. By fostering environments that encourage face-to-face interactions and shared experiences, we can build stronger, more resilient communities where everyone feels valued and included. Moreover, by promoting digital literacy and responsible use of technology, we can harness the power of digital communication to strengthen, rather than undermine, our social connections. Ultimately, by recognizing the importance of human connection in an increasingly digital world, we can create a future where no one feels alone or isolated, but rather supported and connected to a vibrant and thriving community.

Chapter 13: Mental Health Epidemic: Anxiety, Depression, and the Modern Psyche

Mental health has emerged as one of the most pressing public health challenges of our time, with rates of anxiety, depression, and other mental health disorders on the rise around the world. From the stress of juggling work and family responsibilities to the constant pressure to succeed in an increasingly competitive and uncertain world, many of us find ourselves struggling to cope with the demands of modern life, leading to a growing epidemic of mental illness.

At the heart of the mental health epidemic lies the complex interplay of biological, psychological, and social factors that shape the modern psyche. While genetic predispositions and neurobiological factors certainly play a role in the development of mental illness, they are only part of the equation. Environmental stressors, traumatic experiences, and societal pressures also contribute to the onset and exacerbation of mental health disorders, creating a perfect storm of risk factors for individuals living in the modern world.

One of the primary drivers of the mental health epidemic is the relentless pace of modern life, characterized by long work hours, constant connectivity, and a never-ending stream of stimuli. In today's hyper-connected world, we are bombarded with information and expectations from all sides, leaving us feeling overwhelmed and exhausted. Moreover, the pressure to succeed and achieve in every aspect of our lives can lead to feelings of inadequacy and self-doubt, fueling anxiety and depression.

The stigma surrounding mental illness often prevents individuals from seeking help and support when they need it most. In many cultures, mental health issues are still viewed as a sign of weakness or personal failure, leading to shame and social isolation for those who struggle with them. This stigma can prevent people from reaching out for help, leading to delays in diagnosis and treatment and exacerbating the severity of their symptoms.

The lack of access to mental health care services exacerbates the problem, particularly for marginalized and underserved populations. In many communities, mental health care services are scarce or nonexistent, leaving individuals with mental illness to suffer in silence without access to the support and treatment they need. This lack of access to care perpetuates a cycle of suffering and despair, trapping individuals in a cycle of mental illness with no way out.

In confronting the mental health epidemic, it is clear that we must prioritize prevention, early intervention, and access to care for all individuals. By promoting mental health literacy and destigmatizing conversations about mental illness, we can create environments where people feel comfortable seeking help and support when they need it. Moreover, by investing in mental health care services and community support programs, we can ensure that everyone has access to the care and resources they need to thrive. Ultimately, by recognizing the importance of mental health in shaping individual and collective well-being, we can create a future where everyone has the opportunity to live a fulfilling and meaningful life.

Chapter 14: Existential Crises: Navigating Meaning and Purpose in a Consumerist Society

In a consumerist society driven by materialism and consumption, many individuals find themselves grappling with existential questions about the meaning and purpose of life. As we are bombarded with messages that equate happiness and fulfillment with wealth, success, and possessions, we are left wondering whether there is more to life than the pursuit of material wealth and status.

At the heart of the existential crisis lies a fundamental disconnect between our deepest values and aspirations and the values and priorities of consumer culture. In a society that places a premium on external markers of success and identity, such as wealth, status, and possessions, many of us struggle to find meaning and purpose in our lives beyond the pursuit of material wealth and pleasure.

The relentless pursuit of material possessions and status often leads to a sense of emptiness and dissatisfaction, as we discover that wealth and possessions alone are insufficient to fulfill our deepest longings and aspirations. This realization can trigger existential angst and despair, as we grapple with questions about the meaning and purpose of our lives in the face of a culture that values material wealth and consumption above all else.

The pressure to conform to societal expectations and norms can exacerbate feelings of existential crisis, as we feel compelled to live up to unrealistic standards of success and achievement. Whether it's the pressure to climb the corporate ladder, accumulate wealth, or maintain a certain lifestyle, the expectations placed upon us by society can leave us feeling trapped and unfulfilled, as we sacrifice our authenticity and integrity in pursuit of external validation and approval.

In confronting the existential crisis, it is essential that we reclaim our agency and autonomy, charting our own path in pursuit of meaning and purpose. This may involve reevaluating our values and priorities, shifting our focus away from material possessions and external markers of success towards more intrinsic sources of fulfillment, such as personal growth, meaningful relationships, and contributions to the greater good.

It is essential that we cultivate practices of self-reflection and introspection, allowing ourselves the space and time to explore our deepest values, aspirations, and fears. By embracing uncertainty and embracing the unknown, we can cultivate resilience and adaptability in the face of life's inevitable challenges and setbacks, finding meaning and purpose in the journey itself rather than the destination.

Navigating the existential crisis requires courage, authenticity, and a willingness to embrace the uncertainty and complexity of life. By challenging the values and priorities of consumer culture, and cultivating a deeper connection to ourselves, others, and the world around us, we can find meaning and purpose in the midst of the existential crisis, living lives that are rich, meaningful, and fulfilling, regardless of the external circumstances.

Part VI. Resilience and Adaptation: Coping Mechanisms in a Post-Industrial World

Chapter 15: Reconnecting with Nature: The Healing Power of Green Spaces

In the hustle and bustle of modern life, amidst the concrete jungles and towering skyscrapers, it is easy to forget our deep and intrinsic connection to the natural world. Yet, as we become increasingly disconnected from nature, we also become disconnected from ourselves, our sense of well-being, and our understanding of the world around us. In this chapter, we explore the healing power of green spaces and the profound impact that reconnecting with nature can have on our physical, mental, and emotional health.

Green spaces, whether they be expansive parks, lush forests, or serene gardens, have long been recognized for their restorative and rejuvenating qualities. In these natural havens, we find solace from the stresses of daily life, as we immerse ourselves in the sights, sounds, and smells of the natural world. The gentle rustle of leaves in the wind, the melodious chirping of birds, the vibrant colors of flowers in bloom – these sensory experiences awaken our senses and soothe our souls, offering a respite from the frenetic pace of modernity.

Spending time in green spaces has been shown to have tangible benefits for our physical health. Studies have demonstrated that exposure to nature can lower blood pressure, reduce stress levels, and boost immune function. Moreover, spending time outdoors is associated with increased physical activity, as we engage in activities such as walking, hiking, and gardening that promote cardiovascular health and overall well-being.

Green spaces offer unique opportunities for social connection and community engagement. Whether it's gathering with friends for a picnic in the park, participating in a community gardening project, or simply enjoying a leisurely stroll with loved ones, green spaces provide a shared space for people to come together, forge connections, and strengthen social bonds. These social connections are essential for our mental and emotional health, providing support, companionship, and a sense of belonging in an increasingly fragmented and isolating world. Spending time in nature can have profound psychological benefits, helping to reduce symptoms of anxiety, depression, and other mental health disorders. The natural beauty and tranquility of green spaces have a calming effect on the mind, promoting relaxation and mindfulness. Moreover, nature has a way of putting our problems and worries into perspective, reminding us of the vastness and interconnectedness of the world and our place within it.

In confronting the challenges of modern life, it is clear that reconnecting with nature is essential for our health, well-being, and sense of connection to the world around us. By prioritizing the preservation and accessibility of green spaces, we can create environments that promote physical activity, social connection, and mental health for all members of society. Moreover, by cultivating a deeper appreciation for the natural world and our place within it, we can find solace, inspiration, and renewal amidst the beauty and wonder of the great outdoors.

Chapter 16: Digital Detox: Strategies for Reclaiming Balance in the Digital Age

In a time dominated by screens and devices, the constant barrage of digital information and stimuli can overwhelm our senses, leaving us feeling exhausted, anxious, and disconnected from ourselves and the world around us. In this chapter, we explore the concept of digital detoxing and the strategies that we can employ to reclaim balance and well-being in the midst of the digital age.

The first step in embarking on a digital detox is to cultivate awareness of our digital habits and the impact that they have on our lives. This may involve tracking our screen time, monitoring our use of social media and other digital platforms, and reflecting on how our digital habits affect our mood, productivity, and relationships. By becoming more mindful of our digital consumption patterns, we can begin to identify areas where we may be overindulging or engaging in unhealthy behaviors.

Once we have gained awareness of our digital habits, the next step is to set boundaries and limits around our digital use. This may involve establishing designated times and spaces for digital use, such as turning off devices during meals or setting aside specific times of day for checking email and social media. Moreover, we can set limits on the amount of time we spend on digital devices each day, gradually reducing our screen time to more manageable levels.

In addition to setting boundaries around our digital use, it is also important to cultivate alternative activities that promote health and well-being. This may involve spending more time outdoors, engaging in physical activity, practicing mindfulness and meditation, or pursuing hobbies and interests that bring us joy and fulfillment.

By filling our time with meaningful activities that nourish our mind, body, and soul, we can reduce our reliance on digital devices and reconnect with the world around us.

It is important to create digital-free zones and rituals in our daily lives, where we can unplug and disconnect from the digital world. This may involve establishing screen-free bedrooms, implementing digital-free meal times, or incorporating regular digital detox days into our schedules. By carving out dedicated time and space for rest, relaxation, and reflection, we can create opportunities for true connection and presence in our lives. It is essential to cultivate a healthy relationship with technology and digital media, using them as tools for communication, creativity, and learning rather than sources of distraction and stress. This may involve practicing digital mindfulness, being intentional about our use of technology, and seeking out digital content that nourishes and uplifts us rather than depletes and drains us.

Embarking on a digital detox is about reclaiming agency and autonomy over our digital lives, freeing ourselves from the grip of digital addiction and reclaiming balance, well-being, and presence in the digital age. By cultivating awareness, setting boundaries, and prioritizing alternative activities that promote health and well-being, we can create a more balanced and fulfilling relationship with technology, one that supports our overall well-being and enhances our quality of life.

Chapter 17: Cultivating Community: Building Resilient Social Networks in Urban Environments

In the bustling metropolises and urban landscapes of the modern world, it's easy to feel isolated and disconnected from those around us. Yet, amidst the towering skyscrapers and bustling streets, lies the potential for vibrant and resilient communities to thrive. In this chapter, we explore strategies for cultivating community and building resilient social networks in urban environments.

One of the first steps in building resilient social networks in urban environments is to recognize the importance of community and connection in fostering well-being and resilience. Humans are social beings by nature, wired for connection and belonging. Yet, in the fast-paced and transient nature of urban life, meaningful social connections can often be elusive. By acknowledging the importance of community and prioritizing connection in our lives, we can begin to lay the foundation for building resilient social networks in urban environments.

One strategy for cultivating community in urban environments is to create shared spaces and opportunities for social interaction. This may involve establishing community gardens, neighborhood parks, or communal gathering spaces where residents can come together to connect, collaborate, and build relationships. By providing spaces for people to come together and interact, we can foster a sense of belonging and cohesion within urban communities.

It is essential to promote diversity and inclusivity within urban communities, recognizing that diversity is a strength rather than a weakness. By embracing the rich tapestry of cultures, backgrounds, and perspectives that exist within urban environments, we can create more vibrant and resilient communities that are better equipped to adapt and thrive in the face of change.

It is important to foster a culture of reciprocity and mutual support within urban communities, where residents look out for one another and lend a helping hand when needed. This may involve organizing community events, volunteer opportunities, or mutual aid networks where residents can come together to support and uplift one another during times of need. Technology can also play a role in building resilient social networks in urban environments, facilitating connections and fostering a sense of community among residents. Social media platforms, neighborhood apps, and online forums can serve as valuable tools for connecting residents, organizing community events, and sharing resources and information.

Building resilient social networks in urban environments requires a collective effort from residents, community organizations, and local government. By prioritizing community and connection, creating shared spaces for social interaction, promoting diversity and inclusivity, fostering a culture of reciprocity and mutual support, and leveraging technology to facilitate connections, we can create vibrant, resilient, and thriving communities where everyone feels a sense of belonging and connection to those around them.

VII. Towards a Harmonious Future: Reconciling Humanity's Past with its Present

Chapter 18: Sustainable Living: Balancing Technological Progress with Environmental Stewardship

In an age defined by rapid technological advancement and economic growth, the imperative to address environmental challenges and promote sustainable living has never been more urgent. As we stand at the precipice of a climate crisis and ecological collapse, it is clear that we must rethink our approach to technology and development, prioritizing environmental stewardship and sustainability in all aspects of our lives. In this chapter, we explore the concept of sustainable living and the strategies that we can employ to balance technological progress with environmental responsibility.

At the heart of sustainable living lies the recognition that our actions and choices have consequences for the planet and future generations. From the food we eat to the products we consume to the way we travel and commute, every aspect of our daily lives has an environmental impact. By adopting sustainable practices and making conscious choices that minimize our ecological footprint, we can reduce our impact on the environment and promote a more harmonious relationship with the natural world.

One of the key principles of sustainable living is the concept of "reduce, reuse, recycle." By reducing our consumption and minimizing waste, we can conserve natural resources and reduce the amount of pollution and greenhouse gas emissions generated by the production and disposal of goods. Moreover, by reusing and repurposing materials, we can extend the life cycle of products and reduce the demand for new resources. Finally, by recycling and properly disposing of waste, we can minimize the amount of material that ends up in landfills and incinerators, reducing our impact on the environment.

In addition to reducing waste and consumption, sustainable living also involves making conscious choices about the products we consume and the companies we support. By choosing products that are sustainably sourced, produced, and packaged, we can support companies that prioritize environmental stewardship and ethical practices. Moreover, by supporting local businesses and producers, we can reduce the carbon footprint associated with transportation and promote economic resilience within our communities. Sustainable living encompasses practices that promote energy efficiency and conservation. By investing in renewable energy sources such as solar, wind, and hydroelectric power, we can reduce our reliance on fossil fuels and minimize our contribution to climate change. Moreover, by adopting energy-saving practices such as insulating our homes, using energy-efficient appliances, and reducing unnecessary energy consumption, we can lower our energy bills and reduce our impact on the environment.

Sustainable living involves making conscious choices about transportation and mobility. By choosing alternative modes of transportation such as walking, cycling, or public transit, we can reduce our dependence on cars and decrease greenhouse gas emissions associated with transportation. Moreover, by carpooling, ridesharing, and investing in electric or hybrid vehicles, we can further reduce our carbon footprint and promote sustainable mobility solutions.

Sustainable living requires a shift in mindset and behavior, as well as collective action on a global scale. By adopting sustainable practices in our daily lives, supporting companies and policies that prioritize environmental stewardship, and advocating for systemic change, we can create a more sustainable and resilient future for generations to come.

Chapter 19: Human-Centric Design: Creating Spaces and Systems that Nurture Well-Being

Human-centric design is a philosophy that prioritizes the needs, preferences, and experiences of human beings in the design of products, services, and environments. By placing human well-being and satisfaction at the forefront of the design process, human-centric design seeks to create spaces and systems that enhance quality of life, promote health and happiness, and foster a sense of connection and belonging. In this chapter, we explore the principles of human-centric design and the strategies that can be employed to create environments that nurture well-being.

At the heart of human-centric design lies empathy and understanding, as designers seek to gain insight into the needs, desires, and behaviors of the people who will ultimately use and interact with their creations. This may involve conducting user research, observing behavior in real-world settings, and engaging with stakeholders to gain a deeper understanding of their needs and preferences. By empathizing with users and placing ourselves in their shoes, designers can create solutions that truly resonate with and address the needs of their target audience.

One of the key principles of human-centric design is the idea of user-centeredness, which involves involving users in the design process and soliciting their feedback and input throughout the development process. By involving users in co-design workshops, focus groups, and usability testing sessions, designers can ensure that their creations meet the needs and expectations of their target audience and address any pain points or challenges that users may encounter.

Human-centric design also emphasizes the importance of inclusivity and accessibility, ensuring that products, services, and environments are usable and enjoyable by people of all ages, abilities, and backgrounds. This may involve designing for diverse user groups, incorporating universal design principles, and providing alternative formats or accommodations for individuals with disabilities or special needs. By prioritizing inclusivity and accessibility, designers can create solutions that are truly equitable and accessible to all members of society.

Human-centric design also takes into account the holistic well-being of users, considering not only their physical needs but also their emotional, social, and psychological needs. This may involve designing spaces that promote relaxation and stress reduction, incorporating elements of biophilic design to connect users with nature, and fostering opportunities for social interaction and community engagement. By creating environments that support overall well-being, designers can enhance quality of life and promote health and happiness for users.

Human-centric design encourages designers to consider the long-term impact of their creations on the environment and society as a whole. This may involve incorporating sustainable materials and practices into the design process, minimizing waste and pollution, and designing for longevity and durability. By prioritizing environmental sustainability and social responsibility, designers can create solutions that minimize harm to the planet and contribute to a more sustainable and equitable future for all.

Human-centric design is about creating solutions that truly resonate with and enhance the lives of the people who use them. By prioritizing empathy, inclusivity, well-being, and sustainability in the design process, designers can create environments that foster connection, promote health and happiness, and enrich the human experience for generations to come.

Chapter 20: Mindful Consumption: Fostering Consciousness in a Culture of Excess

In a culture that glorifies consumption and materialism, mindful consumption offers a pathway to greater awareness, fulfillment, and sustainability. Rooted in the principles of mindfulness and consciousness, mindful consumption encourages individuals to approach their consumption habits with intentionality, awareness, and consideration for the broader impact on themselves, others, and the planet. In this chapter, we explore the concept of mindful consumption and the strategies that can be employed to foster consciousness in a culture of excess.

At the heart of mindful consumption lies the recognition that our consumption habits have far-reaching consequences for our well-being, our communities, and the environment. By cultivating awareness and mindfulness in our consumption habits, we can make more conscious choices that align with our values, priorities, and goals. This may involve questioning our impulses and desires, reflecting on our true needs and wants, and considering the broader impact of our consumption on society and the planet.

One of the key principles of mindful consumption is the idea of minimalism, which involves simplifying our lives and reducing our reliance on material possessions. By decluttering our spaces, prioritizing quality over quantity, and focusing on experiences rather than things, we can free ourselves from the burden of excess and cultivate greater contentment and fulfillment in our lives. Moreover, by reducing our consumption, we can minimize our environmental footprint and contribute to a more sustainable and equitable world.

Furthermore, mindful consumption encourages individuals to adopt practices that promote conscious decision-making and responsible consumption. This may involve researching the social and environmental impact of products and companies, choosing products that are ethically and sustainably produced, and supporting companies that prioritize transparency and accountability in their business practices. By becoming more informed consumers, we can use our purchasing power to support companies that align with our values and promote positive social and environmental change.

Mindful consumption involves cultivating practices of gratitude and appreciation for the things that we already have. By fostering a mindset of abundance rather than scarcity, we can cultivate greater contentment and satisfaction in our lives, reducing the impulse to constantly seek out new possessions and experiences. Moreover, by appreciating the things that we already have, we can reduce our consumption and minimize our environmental impact, contributing to a more sustainable and balanced way of life.

Mindful consumption is about bringing awareness and consciousness to our consumption habits, recognizing the interconnectedness of all beings and the planet, and making choices that promote well-being and sustainability for ourselves and future generations. By adopting practices of minimalism, responsible consumption, gratitude, and appreciation, we can cultivate a more mindful and fulfilling way of life that prioritizes connection, contentment, and harmony with the world around us.

Part VIII. Conclusion

Chapter 21: Reflections on the Journey: Insights Gained from Exploring Humanity's Psyche

As we journey through the exploration of humanity's psyche, we encounter a myriad of insights, revelations, and reflections that deepen our understanding of ourselves, our society, and our place in the world. From the complexities of post-industrial civilization to the profound impact of technology on human interaction, each aspect of our exploration offers valuable lessons and insights that shed light on the human condition. In this chapter, we reflect on the journey we have embarked upon and the insights gained from our exploration of humanity's psyche.

One of the key insights gained from our exploration is the recognition of the interconnectedness of all aspects of human existence. From our evolutionary legacy to the social and psychological effects of post-industrialism, we see how every facet of human society and behavior is intertwined, shaped by a complex interplay of biological, psychological, and social factors. By understanding these interconnected dynamics, we gain a deeper appreciation for the complexity and richness of the human experience, and the importance of addressing issues holistically rather than in isolation.

Our exploration reveals the profound impact of environmental factors on human well-being and flourishing. From the consequences of urbanization and globalization to the toll of sedentary lifestyles and digital overstimulation, we see how the built environment and technological advancements shape our physical, mental, and emotional health. By recognizing the influence of these external forces on our lives, we can begin to create environments and systems that promote human flourishing and sustainability.

Furthermore, our exploration highlights the importance of fostering connection and community in the digital age. From the challenges of social fragmentation and loneliness to the healing power of green spaces and resilient social networks, we see how human connection is essential for our well-being and resilience. By prioritizing community and fostering meaningful connections with others, we can combat feelings of isolation and alienation and create environments where everyone feels valued, supported, and connected. Our exploration underscores the significance of mindfulness and consciousness in navigating the complexities of modern life. From the practice of digital detoxing to the principles of mindful consumption and human-centric design, we see how mindfulness can help us reclaim agency and autonomy over our lives and cultivate greater well-being and fulfillment. By bringing awareness and intentionality to our thoughts, actions, and choices, we can create lives that are aligned with our values and priorities, and contribute to a more sustainable and compassionate world.

Our journey through the exploration of humanity's psyche reveals the inherent resilience, adaptability, and potential for growth within the human spirit. Despite the challenges and complexities of modern life, we see how individuals and communities have the capacity to overcome adversity, find meaning and purpose, and create positive change in the world. By reflecting on the insights gained from our exploration, we can continue to deepen our understanding of ourselves and our society, and work towards a future that honors the inherent dignity and worth of every human being.

Chapter 22: Charting the Course Forward: Opportunities for Collective Growth and Evolution

As we reflect on our journey through the exploration of humanity's psyche, we are confronted with both the challenges and opportunities that lie ahead. From the complexities of post-industrial civilization to the profound impact of technology on human interaction, our exploration has revealed the interconnectedness of all aspects of human existence and the urgent need for collective action to address the pressing issues facing our world. In this chapter, we chart the course forward and explore the opportunities for collective growth and evolution that can lead us towards a more sustainable, equitable, and fulfilling future.

One of the key opportunities for collective growth and evolution lies in the recognition of our shared humanity and interconnectedness. Despite our differences in culture, background, and belief, we are all members of the human family, bound together by our common humanity and shared aspirations for a better world. By embracing our shared humanity and recognizing the inherent dignity and worth of every individual, we can foster a sense of solidarity and unity that transcends divisions and fosters collaboration towards common goals. Our exploration has revealed the importance of reimagining and redesigning the systems and structures that shape our society. From the way we organize our cities and communities to the way we produce and consume goods and services, there are countless opportunities to create more equitable, sustainable, and resilient systems that promote human flourishing and well-being. By harnessing the power of technology, innovation, and collective action, we can create systems that prioritize the needs of people and the planet and foster a more just and inclusive society for all.

Our exploration has underscored the importance of cultivating resilience and adaptability in the face of change. From the challenges of climate change and environmental degradation to the disruptions caused by technological advancement and globalization, we live in a world that is constantly evolving and changing. By cultivating resilience and adaptability at both the individual and collective levels, we can navigate the complexities of modern life with grace and fortitude, and respond effectively to the challenges and opportunities that arise.

Our exploration has highlighted the importance of fostering a culture of creativity, innovation, and lifelong learning. In a rapidly changing world, the ability to think critically, adapt to new circumstances, and embrace innovation is essential for success and well-being. By investing in education, creativity, and lifelong learning opportunities for all members of society, we can unlock the full potential of every individual and create a future that is rich in possibility and opportunity.

The opportunities for collective growth and evolution are boundless, limited only by our imagination, ingenuity, and commitment to creating a better world. By embracing our shared humanity, reimagining and redesigning our systems and structures, cultivating resilience and adaptability, and fostering a culture of creativity and innovation, we can chart a course towards a future that honors the inherent dignity and worth of every individual and promotes the well-being and flourishing of all members of society.

Chapter 23: Embracing the Complexity: Honoring the Interplay of Human Nature and Post-Industrial Progress

As we navigate the complexities of post-industrial progress, it becomes increasingly clear that our understanding of human nature plays a crucial role in shaping the trajectory of our society. From the evolutionary legacies that influence our behavior to the societal structures that shape our interactions, the interplay between human nature and post-industrial progress is multifaceted and dynamic. In this chapter, we delve into the complexities of this interplay, exploring how an understanding of human nature can inform and enrich our approach to post-industrial progress.

At the heart of the interplay between human nature and post-industrial progress lies an acknowledgment of our evolutionary heritage. As descendants of hunter-gatherer ancestors who roamed the savannas of Africa, we carry with us certain biological predispositions and psychological tendencies that have shaped our behavior for millennia. From our preference for social connection and cooperation to our innate fear of the unknown, these evolutionary legacies continue to influence our behavior and decision-making in the modern world.

Our exploration of human nature reveals the importance of recognizing the complexity and diversity of human experience. While certain universal traits and tendencies may be shared across cultures and societies, there is also tremendous variation in human behavior, preferences, and values. By embracing this diversity and complexity, we can create more inclusive and equitable systems and structures that honor the unique needs and perspectives of all individuals.

Our understanding of human nature can inform our approach to designing environments and systems that promote human flourishing and well-being. By recognizing the importance of social connection, autonomy, and meaning in our lives, we can create environments that foster a sense of belonging, agency, and purpose for all members of society. Moreover, by acknowledging the impact of environmental factors on human health and well-being, we can design cities, communities, and workplaces that support physical, mental, and emotional health for all residents.

Our exploration of human nature reveals the importance of addressing the root causes of societal challenges rather than simply treating symptoms. From the mental health epidemic fueled by social isolation and disconnection to the environmental crises exacerbated by consumerism and overconsumption, many of the challenges facing our world today stem from a disconnect between our innate human needs and the structures of modern society. By addressing these underlying causes and designing systems that align with human nature, we can create a more sustainable, equitable, and resilient future for all.

Embracing the complexity of the interplay between human nature and post-industrial progress requires a willingness to question assumptions, challenge paradigms, and engage in open dialogue and collaboration. By drawing on insights from psychology, anthropology, sociology, and other disciplines, we can deepen our understanding of human nature and its implications for society, and chart a course towards a future that honors the inherent dignity and worth of every individual while promoting the well-being and flourishing of all members of society.

Appendix: Further Readings and Resources

1. "Sapiens: A Brief History of Humankind" by Yuval Noah Harari - This book provides an insightful exploration of human history, from the emergence of Homo sapiens to the present day, offering valuable perspectives on the interplay between human nature and societal progress.

2. "The Sixth Extinction: An Unnatural History" by Elizabeth Kolbert - In this Pulitzer Prize-winning book, Elizabeth Kolbert examines the current mass extinction event and its implications for human civilization, shedding light on the complex relationship between human activity and environmental change.

3. "Digital Minimalism: Choosing a Focused Life in a Noisy World" by Cal Newport - Cal Newport explores the impact of digital technology on human well-being and offers practical strategies for reclaiming control over our digital lives and fostering mindfulness and intentionality in the digital age.

4. "The Nature Fix: Why Nature Makes Us Happier, Healthier, and More Creative" by Florence Williams - Florence Williams explores the restorative power of nature on human health and well-being, offering insights into the psychological and physiological benefits of spending time in natural environments.

5. "Cradle to Cradle: Remaking the Way We Make Things" by William McDonough and Michael Braungart - This groundbreaking book presents a vision for a sustainable and regenerative approach to design and production, offering practical strategies for creating products and systems that mimic the cycles of nature.

6. "Lost Connections: Uncovering the Real Causes of Depression – and the Unexpected Solutions" by Johann Hari - Johann Hari explores the root causes of depression and anxiety in modern society, challenging conventional wisdom and offering alternative perspectives on mental health and well-being.

7. "The Art of Happiness" by Dalai Lama XIV and Howard C. Cutler - In this classic book, the Dalai Lama shares insights into the nature of happiness and offers practical advice for cultivating inner peace, contentment, and fulfillment in everyday life.

8. "Braiding Sweetgrass: Indigenous Wisdom, Scientific Knowledge, and the Teachings of Plants" by Robin Wall Kimmerer - Robin Wall Kimmerer weaves together indigenous wisdom, scientific knowledge, and personal narrative to explore the interconnectedness of all living beings and the importance of reciprocity and stewardship in our relationship with the natural world.

9. "Designing Your Life: How to Build a Well-Lived, Joyful Life" by Bill Burnett and Dave Evans - Bill Burnett and Dave Evans offer a practical framework for designing a life that is meaningful, fulfilling, and aligned with one's values and aspirations, drawing on principles of design thinking and creativity.

10. "The Social Animal: The Hidden Sources of Love, Character, and Achievement" by David Brooks - David Brooks delves into the complexities of human behavior and social interaction, offering insights into the factors that shape our relationships, choices, and destinies.

These resources provide valuable insights and perspectives on the topics explored in this book, offering further avenues for exploration and reflection on the interplay between human nature and post-industrial progress. Whether you are interested in psychology, sociology, environmental science, or personal development, these readings offer valuable perspectives and insights that can deepen your understanding of the complexities of the human experience and inform your approach to navigating the challenges and opportunities of the modern world.

Styles Stagnation
Cultural Hibernation

Julian Del Bel

Chapter 1: The Era of Rapid Change
- The Fashion and Cultural Evolution: 1940s-1980s
- Key Societal Shifts and Their Impact on Culture and Style
- Summary of Pre-Hibernation Dynamics
- Introduction to Cultural Hibernation

Chapter 2: Entering Cultural Hibernation
- The Late 90s and Early 00s: A Transition Period
- Defining Cultural Hibernation
- Technological Advancements and Their Dual-Edged Impact

Chapter 3: Fashion's Slow Dance
- The Illusion of Change: Fast Fashion and Micro Trends
- Core Staples: A Comparison of Then and Now
- The Role of Media and Celebrity Influence

Chapter 4: The Technological Cocoon
- From Connectivity to Isolation
- Social Media: The Mirror and the Mirage
- The Digital Divide and Its Cultural Consequences

Chapter 5: Victor Frankl and Cultural Stagnation
- Overview of Frankl's Theory and Its Relevance

- Prisoners' Cultural Hibernation: Parallels in Modern Society
- Lessons from Logotherapy for a Stagnant Culture

Chapter 6: The Impact of Cultural Hibernation
- Psychological Effects of Stagnation and Isolation
- Creativity and Innovation: The Lost Art
- The Environmental Toll of Fast Fashion

Chapter 7: Awakening from Hibernation
- Signs of Emerging from Cultural Stagnation
- The Role of Individual and Collective Action
- Embracing Change and Authenticity

Chapter 8: The Future of Fashion and Culture
- Predictions and Possibilities
- Technology: A Tool for Liberation or Further Isolation?
- Reimagining a Culturally Dynamic Society

Conclusion
- Summary of Key Insights
- Call to Action: Breaking Free from Cultural Hibernation

Appendices
- Timeline of Fashion and Cultural Changes: 1940s-2020s
- Further Reading and Resources

Foreword

In the vast expanse of human history, culture has been the mirror reflecting our collective soul, continuously evolving in response to the ebb and flow of societal currents. Yet, as we navigated the turn of the millennium, a subtle shift occurred—a slowing of the cultural pulse that once beat so vigorously at the heart of innovation and creativity. This book delves into the phenomenon of cultural hibernation, a period marked by a seeming stagnation in the realms of fashion, art, and societal values, and offers a roadmap for awakening from this slumber.

As we explore the pages within, we are invited to examine the forces that have led us into this state of hibernation, from the rapid technological advancements that promised connection but delivered isolation, to the fast fashion trends that emphasized quantity over quality. Through a careful analysis of the past and present, the book illuminates the paths by which we might emerge into a future where culture thrives on authenticity, diversity, and sustainability.

This foreword serves as an invitation to readers to embark on a journey of exploration and discovery. It is a call to action for individuals and communities alike to participate in the shaping of a vibrant cultural landscape, one that cherishes innovation and creativity as the pillars upon which society stands.

As you turn these pages, may you find inspiration, insight, and the courage to contribute to a cultural renaissance that transcends the limitations of our time, forging a legacy of richness and depth for generations to come.

Chapter 1: The Era of Rapid Change

The Fashion and Cultural Evolution: 1940s-1980s

The span from the 1940s to the 1980s was a period of intense cultural and fashion evolution, mirroring the seismic shifts in society, technology, and global politics. Unlike any other time in history, each decade within this forty-year stretch presented a distinct aesthetic and cultural ethos, directly influenced by the broader socio-economic landscape, technological advancements, and shifting cultural attitudes. This era was marked by a cycle of post-war reconstruction, economic booms and recessions, social revolutions, and the onset of the digital age, each leaving an indelible mark on the world of fashion and culture.

1940s: Post-War Elegance and Austerity

The decade immediately following World War II was characterized by a mix of austerity and opulence. Fabric rationing imposed during the war years led to the creation of styles that were both practical and elegant, epitomized by the "Utility clothing" in Britain. Despite these constraints, the late 1940s saw a dramatic shift with the introduction of Christian Dior's "New Look" in 1947, characterized by cinched waists, voluminous skirts, and a silhouette that celebrated femininity—a stark contrast to wartime austerity. This period laid the groundwork for the fashion industry's recovery, setting the stage for the extravagant explorations of identity and style that would define subsequent decades.

1950s: Prosperity and Conformity

The post-war economic boom of the 1950s fostered a culture of prosperity and conformity in the West. Fashion during this era reflected the societal return to traditional gender roles, with women's fashion emphasizing curves and femininity through full skirts and fitted waists, and men's fashion showcasing a clean, tailored look. The rise of consumer culture also saw the birth of teen fashion as a distinct category, with the younger generation beginning to assert their identities and preferences in the cultural landscape. Icons like Marilyn Monroe, with her glamorous and seductive style, and James Dean, embodying the cool rebel, became style symbols, influencing fashion in profound ways.

1960s: Cultural Revolution and Freedom

The 1960s were a decade of upheaval and transformation, challenging established norms and conventions. This era witnessed the flowering of the civil rights movement, the feminist movement, and anti-Vietnam War protests, each contributing to a broader cultural revolution. Fashion became a powerful medium for expressing solidarity, dissent, and desire for change. The miniskirt, popularized by Mary Quant, became a symbol of female liberation, while the psychedelic prints and unisex garments of the late '60s reflected the era's spirit of freedom and experimentation. The decade also marked the rise of the counterculture, with the hippie movement adopting ethnic-inspired styles, promoting peace, love, and communal living.

1970s: Disco and Diversity

The 1970s unfolded with an explosion of diversity and experimentation in fashion, mirroring the decade's eclectic musical landscape from glam rock to disco. The early '70s saw the continuation of the hippie aesthetic, with an emphasis on natural materials and ethnic patterns. However, as the decade progressed, fashion took a turn towards the extravagant and theatrical, epitomized by the disco culture's sequined dresses, satin shirts, and bell-bottom pants. This era was also marked by the punk movement, which challenged the disco's flamboyance with its own gritty, rebellious style featuring leather jackets, ripped jeans, and aggressive accessories, emphasizing an anti-establishment ethos.

1980s: Excess and Individuality

The 1980s were characterized by bold statements in fashion and a pronounced emphasis on individuality and excess. Economic prosperity fueled a culture of consumption, reflected in the popularity of luxury brands and the "power dressing" phenomenon. Women's fashion incorporated shoulder pads and bold prints, signaling strength and ambition, while men's fashion saw the rise of the yuppie, characterized by designer suits and an air of sophistication. Cultural icons of the era, including Madonna, Michael Jackson, and Prince, pushed the boundaries of gender and fashion, fostering a climate of experimentation and self-expression.

Key Societal Shifts and Their Impact on Culture and Style

This period of rapid evolution in fashion was deeply intertwined with key societal shifts. Post-war reconstruction efforts and subsequent economic booms facilitated a surge in consumer spending, including on fashion. Technological innovations, particularly in textile manufacturing and media, transformed how fashion was produced and consumed. The introduction of television and the expansion of mass media brought fashion icons and trends into living rooms around the world, amplifying their influence on public style.

Changes in societal attitudes, especially those concerning gender roles and civil rights, also played a crucial role. The feminist movement of the 1960s and 1970s, for example, not only fought for women's rights but also challenged traditional notions of femininity and masculinity, directly influencing fashion trends and the industry's approach to gender. Similarly, the civil rights movement and the push for racial equality introduced elements of African American culture into mainstream fashion, enriching it with new textures, colors, and patterns.

Pre-Hibernation Dynamics

The decades leading up to the cultural hibernation of the late 1990s and early 2000s were marked by a whirlwind of change and diversity in fashion and culture. This period was characterized by a vibrant exploration of identity, style, and social norms, propelled by economic shifts, technological advancements, and a spirit of rebellion and experimentation. However, as the new millennium approached, this rapid pace of change began to slow, transitioning into a period of cultural hibernation. In contrast to the dynamic transformations of previous decades, the late 1990s and early 2000s saw a stagnation in fashion innovation, with trends recycling past styles rather than introducing new paradigms.

Introduction to Cultural Hibernation

Cultural hibernation signifies a period where significant shifts in fashion, style, and culture become less frequent or impactful, leading to a state of stagnation or minimal evolution. This book posits that the transition into the 21st century marked the beginning of such a period, characterized by a recycling of past trends and a notable decrease in the emergence of groundbreaking cultural phenomena. The concept of cultural hibernation serves as a lens through which we can examine the factors contributing to this stagnation, including technological isolation and the saturation of ideas and styles. Drawing parallels with Victor Frankl's observations of prisoners' psychological states, this chapter lays the groundwork for a deeper exploration of the modern cultural landscape, questioning the implications of our self-imposed isolation and the paths to awakening from our cultural slumber.

Chapter 2: Entering Cultural Hibernation

As we transition from the whirlwind of change characteristic of the mid-20th century to the seemingly more stable yet complex cultural landscape of the late 1990s and early 2000s, we find ourselves at the cusp of what this book terms "cultural hibernation." This chapter explores the transition into this period of cultural hibernation, focusing on its defining characteristics, the impact of technological advancements, and the paradoxical effects of these developments on culture and fashion.

The Late 90s and Early 00s: A Transition Period

The late 1990s and early 2000s served as a pivotal transition period, marking a shift from the rapid cultural and stylistic evolutions of previous decades to a new era where changes in fashion and culture appeared to slow down. This period was characterized by the emergence of the internet and digital technology as central to daily life, altering how people interacted with each other and consumed culture. The global economy also saw significant changes, with the dot-com boom and subsequent bust shaping economic and cultural landscapes.

In fashion, this era was marked by a blend of minimalism and the resurgence of past styles. The grunge trend of the early '90s slowly gave way to a more polished and simplistic aesthetic, while the late '90s and early 2000s saw the revival of '70s and '80s fashion elements, such as flared pants, crop tops, and platform shoes, albeit in a more subdued form. This recycling of past trends rather than the creation of new ones suggested an initial sign of cultural hibernation.

Defining Cultural Hibernation

Cultural hibernation can be understood as a period of reduced innovation and creativity within the cultural and fashion industries, where changes become incremental rather than revolutionary. This phase is characterized by a significant slowdown in the emergence of new styles, artistic movements, and cultural norms, leading to a landscape dominated by nostalgia and the rehashing of previous trends. Unlike the dynamic shifts witnessed in earlier decades, cultural hibernation embodies a period where society seems to rest, contemplate, and perhaps unconsciously wait for the next wave of cultural upheaval.

This hibernation does not imply a complete cessation of cultural production or fashion evolution but indicates a relative lack of groundbreaking developments. The causes of cultural hibernation are multifaceted, encompassing economic factors, technological advancements, and shifts in societal values and behaviors. It reflects a moment in time when the cultural momentum of previous eras appears to plateau, leading to a more introspective and reflective phase in the cultural zeitgeist.

Technological Advancements and Their Dual-Edged Impact

The late 20th and early 21st centuries were defined by rapid technological advancements, particularly in the realm of digital technology and the internet. These innovations transformed every aspect of daily life, including how people communicated, worked, and engaged with culture. The democratization of access to information and the globalization of cultural exchange were among the most significant outcomes, with the internet allowing for an unprecedented flow of ideas and influences across borders.

However, this technological revolution had a dual-edged impact on culture and fashion. On one hand, it facilitated a broader dissemination and accessibility of fashion and cultural products, enabling individuals around the globe to partake in trends and movements instantaneously. This connectivity fostered a sense of global community and shared cultural experiences, breaking down geographic and cultural barriers.

On the other hand, the saturation of the market with information and the constant bombardment of media led to a dilution of the impact of new trends and ideas. The overwhelming abundance of choices and influences contributed to a sense of cultural overload, where nothing seemed truly novel or groundbreaking. Furthermore, the ease of accessing and replicating past styles through digital archives contributed to the recycling of trends and a nostalgia-driven culture, reinforcing the state of cultural hibernation.

The proliferation of digital platforms also shifted the fashion industry's dynamics, with social media emerging as a powerful tool for brand marketing and consumer engagement. While this democratized fashion and allowed for more diverse voices and perspectives, it also led to the homogenization of styles and the rapid commodification of trends, further contributing to the stagnation of genuine innovation.

In sum, the transition into cultural hibernation at the turn of the millennium was influenced by a complex interplay of technological advancements, economic shifts, and changing societal attitudes. The dual-edged impact of technology—both connecting and overwhelming—played a pivotal role in shaping this period of cultural introspection and repetition. As we look deeper into the nuances of cultural hibernation, we must consider how these factors combined to create a landscape ripe for eventual renewal and resurgence, setting the stage for the cultural awakenings explored in subsequent chapters.

Chapter 3: Fashion's Slow Dance

In the tapestry of cultural evolution, fashion holds a unique place, mirroring societal changes, technological advancements, and shifts in collective consciousness. However, the period from the late 1990s into the new millennium marked a noticeable deceleration in the pace of innovation within the fashion industry, a phenomenon we term as cultural hibernation. This chapter looks into the intricate dance of fashion during this era, characterized by the illusion of change, the persistence of core staples, and the significant impact of media and celebrity influence.

The Illusion of Change: Fast Fashion and Micro Trends

As the 21st century unfolded, the fashion industry experienced a paradoxical trend: while the number of fashion cycles increased, the genuine innovation in design and style began to wane. This period saw the rise of fast fashion, a business model predicated on the rapid production and turnover of inexpensive clothing, designed to cater to the latest trends with minimal lead time. Brands like Zara, H&M, and Forever 21 democratized access to trendy clothing, allowing consumers to partake in the latest fashion trends at a fraction of the cost associated with designer labels.

However, this acceleration of fashion cycles did not equate to a diversification of creativity. Instead, it led to the proliferation of micro-trends—short-lived trends with a rapid rise and fall within a single season or year. These trends created an illusion of constant change and novelty, yet often lacked depth or genuine innovation, recycling and reiterating past styles with minor variations. This phenomenon contributed to the sense of cultural hibernation, where the surface appearance of constant evolution masked a deeper stagnation in originality and creativity.

Core Staples: A Comparison of Then and Now

Despite the rapid turnover of trends, certain core staples have persisted through the decades, serving as a bridge between past and present fashion landscapes. These staples—such as the little black dress, denim jeans, and leather jackets—have endured the test of time, adapting to subtle shifts in style but remaining fundamentally unchanged in their essence.

The late '90s and early '00s, in particular, showcased a resurgence of '70s and '80s fashion staples, reinterpreted with a contemporary twist. For example, flared jeans and platform shoes, hallmarks of the '70s disco era, made a comeback, albeit in more refined and subdued forms. Similarly, the punk-inspired elements of the '80s, such as ripped denim and leather, were reintegrated into mainstream fashion, reflecting a nostalgic yet modern aesthetic.

This persistence of core staples highlights a key aspect of cultural hibernation in fashion: the reliance on familiar, timeless elements as anchors in a sea of fleeting trends. While these staples provide a sense of continuity and stability, their enduring presence also underscores the industry's cautious approach to innovation during this period, favoring the safe appeal of the known over the risks of the new.

The Role of Media and Celebrity Influence

The impact of media and celebrity influence on fashion cannot be overstated, particularly in the context of cultural hibernation. The late '90s and early '00s witnessed an explosion in the accessibility of media, fueled by the advent of the internet, social media platforms, and the 24-hour news cycle. Celebrities and influencers emerged as pivotal figures in the fashion landscape, wielding significant power over trends and consumer preferences.

Fashion icons of the era, such as Sarah Jessica Parker, Jennifer Lopez, and Britney Spears, became trendsetters, their personal styles closely emulated by the public. The media's relentless coverage of celebrity fashion—on the red carpet, in music videos, and in paparazzi shots—played a crucial role in shaping public perceptions of what was fashionable or desirable. This phenomenon contributed to the rapid dissemination and saturation of micro-trends, as consumers sought to replicate the styles of their favorite celebrities, further accelerating the cycle of fast fashion.

Moreover, the rise of reality television and celebrity-driven content provided a new platform for fashion exposure, blurring the lines between high fashion and streetwear, and between personal style and branded marketing. This symbiotic relationship between fashion, media, and celebrity culture amplified the visibility of trends but also contributed to their ephemeral nature, reinforcing the cycle of cultural hibernation by prioritizing immediate appeal over lasting innovation.

The early 21st century's fashion landscape reveals a complex interplay of factors contributing to the phenomenon of cultural hibernation. The illusion of constant change masked by fast fashion and micro-trends, the enduring appeal of core staples, and the significant influence of media and celebrities together created a period of seeming stagnation beneath the surface dynamism. This "slow dance" of fashion, characterized by subtle shifts rather than bold strides, reflects a broader cultural hesitancy to venture into uncharted territories, opting instead for the comforting familiarity of the known and the nostalgic allure of the past.

Chapter 4: The Technological Cocoon

As we ventured into the 21st century, the digital revolution promised an era of unprecedented connectivity, with the internet and mobile technologies heralding new ways of interacting, sharing, and learning. Yet, as this chapter looks deeper into the fabric of our digital existence, it becomes apparent that these advancements, while knitting us closer in some respects, have also spun a cocoon of isolation and superficial engagement around us, impacting cultural evolution and contributing to the phenomenon of cultural hibernation.

From Connectivity to Isolation

The early promises of digital technology centered around the idea of a global village, where people from all corners of the earth could connect, share ideas, and foster understanding. Initially, the impact was profoundly positive, facilitating movements, empowering marginalized voices, and creating a new landscape for cultural and social interaction.

However, as digital platforms proliferated, the quality of these connections began to diminish. The ease of digital communication led to an unexpected consequence: a decline in real-world interactions and community engagement. Physical spaces for communal activity and cultural exchange, such as community centers, libraries, and local art venues, saw reduced participation as individuals turned increasingly towards online forums and social networks for interaction.

This shift towards digital engagement brought about a paradoxical sense of isolation. The constant presence of others in our digital lives, paradoxically, made genuine connections feel more distant. The depth of relationships was often sacrificed for breadth, leading to a landscape where many felt connected to all but closely tied to few. This isolation, occurring within the crowded digital sphere, has had profound implications for cultural growth and exchange, as the nuanced, complex interactions that spur innovation and cultural evolution became rarer.

Social Media: The Mirror and the Mirage

Social media platforms, integral to the digital age, have served as both a mirror reflecting our desires for connection and recognition and a mirage, presenting an illusionary world of endless happiness and success. These platforms became the stage for a curated presentation of life, where the complexities, struggles, and mundane realities were often obscured behind a veneer of perfection.

This curated reality created a culture of comparison, where individuals measured their own lives against the idealized images presented by others, often leading to dissatisfaction and a sense of inadequacy. The pressure to maintain this digital facade detracted from the authenticity and depth of personal expression, with significant consequences for cultural and artistic innovation. In a world where the appearance of success often outweighed genuine creative achievement, cultural production became more about adherence to popular trends and less about pushing boundaries or exploring new ideas.

Moreover, the algorithms governing these platforms exacerbated this issue by creating echo chambers that reinforced existing preferences and views, limiting exposure to diverse ideas and perspectives. This homogenization of cultural consumption not only stifled individual creativity but also narrowed the collective cultural imagination, anchoring society more firmly within the bounds of cultural hibernation.

The Digital Divide and Its Cultural Consequences

The advent of the digital age also highlighted significant disparities in access to technology, leading to the emergence of the digital divide. This divide separates those with easy access to digital technologies and the internet from those without, creating disparities in information access, economic opportunities, and cultural participation. The consequences of the digital divide are multifaceted, affecting not only economic and educational outcomes but also the diversity and richness of cultural expression.

Communities and individuals on the disadvantaged side of the digital divide find themselves increasingly marginalized from mainstream cultural narratives, which are predominantly shaped and shared through digital platforms. This exclusion contributes to a cultural landscape that lacks diversity, as the voices and experiences of a significant portion of the global population are underrepresented or absent. The resultant monoculture not only impoverishes the cultural dialogue but also reinforces the stagnation characteristic of cultural hibernation, as innovation often springs from the collision and amalgamation of diverse perspectives and experiences.

Navigating the Cocoon: Toward a More Connected Future

The technological cocoon of the early 21st century, for all its promises of connectivity, has in many ways isolated us from one another and from the depth of engagement necessary for true cultural evolution. To emerge from this state of cultural hibernation, a conscious effort is required to penetrate the cocoon and reclaim the richness of human connection and cultural exchange.

This effort involves recognizing the value of face-to-face interactions, fostering communities that encourage real-world engagement, and creating spaces for diverse voices and perspectives. It also necessitates a critical examination of our digital habits, promoting a culture of authenticity over perfection, and valuing depth over breadth in our connections. By navigating these challenges, society can leverage the positive aspects of digital technology while mitigating its isolating effects, paving the way for a cultural renaissance in the digital age.

Chapter 5: Victor Frankl and Cultural Stagnation

In examining the phenomenon of cultural hibernation through the lens of Victor Frankl's existential psychology, we uncover a profound narrative about the quest for meaning amidst the trappings of modern societal constructs. Frankl's work, particularly his foundational text *Man's Search for Meaning* and his development of logotherapy, provides essential insights into understanding the underpinnings of cultural stagnation and offers a beacon for navigating out of this existential malaise.

Overview of Frankl's Theory and Its Relevance

Victor Frankl articulated a profound understanding of human resilience and the quest for meaning through his observations and experiences in Nazi concentration camps. His existential analysis, encapsulated in logotherapy, posits that the fundamental drive in human beings is not pleasure (as Freud suggested) nor power (as Adler argued), but rather the pursuit of what he termed "meaning." Frankl's experiences led him to conclude that individuals could endure suffering and find a reason to continue living if they had a purpose or meaning to their lives.

The relevance of Frankl's theory to our discussion lies in his identification of the "existential vacuum," a condition of meaninglessness that he saw as a malaise of modern society. This condition is characterized by a lack of direction and purpose, which Frankl observed was becoming increasingly prevalent. The parallels between this existential vacuum and the phenomenon of cultural hibernation are striking; both are defined by a pervasive sense of aimlessness and a dearth of genuine innovation or progression.

Prisoners' Cultural Hibernation: Parallels in Modern Society

Frankl's concept of the existential vacuum mirrors the stagnation observed in contemporary culture, where a superficial abundance of choice and connectivity masks a deeper paucity of meaningful engagement and creativity. This cultural hibernation, akin to the psychological state Frankl observed among his fellow prisoners, arises not from a lack of resources or freedom but from a loss of direction and purpose. The prisoners, despite their dire circumstances, found solace and strength in their inner values, personal connections, and hopes for the future. Similarly, our society, awash with technological advancements and material wealth, faces the challenge of finding meaning beyond the immediate gratification of consumerism and digital escapism.

In the context of cultural hibernation, this loss of meaning manifests in a cycle of repetitive trends, where innovation is often sacrificed for the comfort of the familiar. The relentless pursuit of novelty in fashion, art, and media, driven by the economic imperatives of the market, often leads to a recycling of ideas rather than the cultivation of new ones. This cycle not only stifles genuine creativity but also contributes to a sense of disconnection and ennui among individuals, who are constantly bombarded with stimuli yet starved for real engagement and purpose.

Lessons from Logotherapy for a Stagnant Culture

Frankl's logotherapy offers several pathways for transcending the existential vacuum and, by extension, cultural stagnation. Central to logotherapy is the belief that meaning can be found in every moment of living, even in the most miserable of circumstances, and that it is the individual's responsibility to seek out this meaning.

1. Intentionality and Choice: Frankl emphasized the importance of living intentionally, making conscious choices that align with one's values and aspirations. Culturally, this suggests a shift towards more mindful consumption and creation, where individuals and communities actively choose to engage with works that challenge, inspire, and provoke thought rather than passively accepting the status quo.

2. Transcendence Through Creativity: For Frankl, creativity was a key pathway to finding meaning, allowing individuals to transcend their circumstances by contributing something unique to the world. Encouraging a culture that values and supports diverse creative expressions can serve as an antidote to stagnation, fostering an environment where innovation can flourish.

3. Future Orientation: Frankl posited that a focus on future goals and possibilities could provide the motivation needed to endure current suffering. Similarly, envisioning a future where culture thrives on genuine innovation and connection can motivate society to break free from the cycles of hibernation, setting ambitious collective goals for cultural achievement.

4. Community and Connectivity: Finally, Frankl highlighted the importance of genuine human connections and community in finding meaning. In the age of digital isolation, fostering real-world communities that celebrate cultural diversity and encourage meaningful interactions can counterbalance the effects of the technological cocoon, revitalizing the cultural landscape.

In essence, Victor Frankl's insights into the human search for meaning offer a powerful framework for addressing the root causes of cultural stagnation. By embracing intentionality, creativity, a forward-looking perspective, and deepening community connections, society can begin to emerge from its state of hibernation, rediscovering the joy and purpose in cultural innovation and shared human experience.

Chapter 6: The Impact of Cultural Hibernation

As we look deeper into the ramifications of cultural hibernation, it becomes clear that this phenomenon has profound implications not only for the arts and media but also for society at large. The pervasive stagnation and isolation intrinsic to this period have psychological effects, stifle creativity and innovation, and exert a heavy environmental toll, particularly through the lens of the fast fashion industry. This chapter examines these impacts in greater detail, exploring the broader consequences of a culture in stasis.

Psychological Effects of Stagnation and Isolation

The psychological landscape of cultural hibernation is marked by a complex interplay of stagnation and isolation, yielding a multifaceted spectrum of effects on individual and collective well-being. The relentless pace of digital life, combined with the superficiality of online interactions and the echo chambers of social media, has fostered a sense of disconnection from the tangible world and from meaningful human experiences. This digital isolation, juxtaposed with an overwhelming abundance of content that lacks depth, contributes to a pervasive sense of ennui—a feeling of listlessness and dissatisfaction arising from a lack of excitement, purpose, or meaning.

Moreover, the phenomenon of cultural hibernation, with its recycling of trends and ideas, can lead to a diminished sense of identity and personal authenticity. Individuals navigating this landscape often find themselves mirroring the transient preferences and styles dictated by media and peers, leading to an erosion of personal uniqueness and a crisis of self. This crisis is compounded by the paradoxical nature of digital connectivity, which, while offering unprecedented access to information and networks, often results in a shallower understanding of the world and a weaker sense of belonging.

The mental health implications are significant. Rates of anxiety, depression, and loneliness have been observed to rise, correlating with the increasing dominance of digital interactions and the continuous bombardment of media. The erosion of community and the dwindling of shared cultural experiences that resonate on a deeper, more meaningful level exacerbate these issues, underscoring the urgent need for a cultural renaissance that champions genuine connection, creativity, and innovation.

Creativity and Innovation: The Lost Art

Cultural hibernation represents a profound crisis in creativity and innovation. In an era where the new quickly becomes old and where novelty is often superficial, the intrinsic value of creative risk-taking and groundbreaking innovation is undermined. The arts, literature, music, and even scientific research face pressures to conform to market demands, prioritizing short-term engagement and profitability over long-term value and impact. This commodification of culture results in a landscape littered with remakes, sequels, and works that iterate on existing formulas rather than breaking new ground.

This stagnation in creativity is not merely an artistic concern but a societal one, impacting everything from education to industry. When cultural outputs become homogenized, the ability of society to foster critical thinking, empathy, and innovation is compromised. Creativity is a crucial driver of progress, offering new perspectives and solutions to complex problems. Its decline signals a broader cultural malaise, where the pursuit of quick returns stifles the growth of ideas that have the potential to inspire change and propel society forward.

The Environmental Toll of Fast Fashion

The environmental impact of cultural hibernation is nowhere more visible than in the fast fashion industry, which stands as a stark symbol of the unsustainable practices that have become normalized in consumer culture. Fast fashion epitomizes the relentless cycle of consumption and disposal that characterizes cultural hibernation, with new trends emerging and fading with dizzying speed, driven by the incessant demand for novelty at low costs.

The consequences for the planet are dire. The fashion industry is a major contributor to water pollution, carbon emissions, and textile waste, with billions of garments produced annually, only to be discarded after a few wears. This wastefulness is emblematic of the broader environmental degradation facilitated by a culture that values immediacy and disposability over sustainability and mindfulness.

Moreover, the fast fashion model has social implications, often relying on exploitative labor practices to meet demand. This raises ethical concerns about the cost of cultural stagnation—not just in terms of environmental damage but in human terms, highlighting the need for a shift towards more sustainable, ethical, and innovative practices in fashion and beyond.

In sum, the impact of cultural hibernation extends deep into the fabric of society, manifesting in psychological distress, a stifling of creative and innovative potential, and environmental degradation. Overcoming this state of cultural stasis requires a concerted effort to foster genuine connections, champion creativity and innovation, and embrace sustainability. As we look to the future, the challenge lies in awakening from this hibernation to cultivate a culture that values depth, meaning, and responsibility to the planet and to each other.

Chapter 7: Awakening from Hibernation

As we navigate through the depths of cultural hibernation, there emerges a glimmer of hope—a series of signs indicating a collective awakening from the stagnation that has ensnared society's creative spirit. This chapter delves into these harbingers of renewal, the pivotal role of individual and collective action in catalyzing change, and the essential embrace of change and authenticity as cornerstones for a vibrant future.

Signs of Emerging from Cultural Stagnation

A key indicator of emergence from cultural stagnation is the renewed interest in traditional crafts and art forms. Across the globe, communities are turning back to their roots, rediscovering and revitalizing age-old practices that speak volumes of their heritage and history. This resurgence is not merely an act of preservation but a bold statement of identity in an increasingly homogenized world. It represents a collective yearning for depth and meaning, a counter-movement to the disposable culture that has dominated recent decades.

Grassroots Movements and Local Initiatives

Another sign of awakening is the proliferation of grassroots movements and local initiatives aimed at fostering cultural enrichment and community engagement. From urban gardening projects that reclaim public spaces for communal art installations to independent bookstores hosting local authors and artists, these initiatives reflect a growing desire to cultivate shared experiences and narratives that resonate with community values and aspirations. Such movements, often driven by the younger generation, signal a shift towards a more participatory and inclusive cultural landscape.

Digital Platforms for Niche and Independent Creators

The rise of digital platforms dedicated to niche and independent creators is also indicative of a departure from mainstream, mass-produced content. These platforms offer a space for diverse voices and unconventional stories, challenging the status quo and broadening the cultural horizon. By democratizing access to the tools of production and distribution, technology has empowered a new wave of creators to share their visions with a global audience, fostering a dynamic and multifaceted cultural ecosystem.

The Role of Individual and Collective Action

The journey out of cultural hibernation begins with the individual—a recognition of one's agency in shaping the cultural milieu. Each choice, from the art we consume to the products we purchase, contributes to the broader cultural narrative. By consciously supporting ethical and sustainable practices, championing diversity, and engaging with content that challenges and inspires, individuals can drive demand for a richer, more authentic cultural landscape.

Collective Mobilization and Advocacy

While individual actions are crucial, it is collective mobilization and advocacy that wield the power to effect systemic change. By coming together to support cultural institutions, advocate for policies that promote cultural diversity and sustainability, and invest in community-driven projects, society can create an environment where creativity and innovation flourish. Collective action can also challenge and dismantle the structures that perpetuate cultural homogenization, paving the way for a more vibrant and inclusive cultural expression.

Embracing Change and Authenticity

Emerging from cultural hibernation requires the courage to embrace change—not as a force to be feared but as an opportunity for growth and renewal. This entails letting go of outdated models and narratives that no longer serve society, opening up to new ideas, and experimenting with alternative ways of thinking and being. Embracing change means acknowledging that culture is not static but a living, breathing entity that evolves with us.

Authenticity as a Guiding Principle

At the heart of this awakening is the principle of authenticity—a return to what is genuine, meaningful, and true. In a world saturated with superficiality and pretense, authenticity stands as a beacon of integrity, urging individuals and communities to forge connections that transcend the superficial and engage with the world in a manner that is honest and heartfelt. By valuing authenticity in all aspects of cultural expression, society can cultivate an environment that nurtures true creativity and innovation, fostering a cultural renaissance that celebrates the richness of the human experience.

The path out of cultural hibernation is illuminated by signs of an emerging renaissance, driven by the revival of traditional crafts, grassroots initiatives, and the rise of digital platforms for independent creators. The journey forward demands both individual responsibility and collective action, underpinned by a steadfast commitment to embracing change and championing authenticity. Together, these elements form the cornerstone of a society poised to awaken from its slumber, ready to reimagine and reinvent its cultural legacy for future generations.

Chapter 7.5: Awakening from Hibernation

Emerging from the depths of cultural hibernation calls for a collective reimagining and revitalization of the societal fabric that binds us. This chapter delves into the nuanced strategies and insights necessary to catalyze a renaissance in creativity and innovation, breaking free from the grips of stagnation and isolation that have characterized the cultural landscape in recent years.

Overcoming Cultural Stagnation: Insights and Strategies

The journey out of cultural stagnation is multifaceted, requiring a concerted effort across various sectors and disciplines. It is a journey that demands a return to authenticity, a commitment to fostering innovation, and a reevaluation of the role of technology in our lives.

Cultivating a Culture of Authenticity and Depth

The antidote to a culture of repetition and superficiality is the cultivation of authenticity and depth in personal and communal expressions. This involves valuing stories, traditions, and creative endeavors that resonate with genuine human experiences and emotions. Encouraging artists, writers, filmmakers, and creators to delve into narratives that challenge conventional norms and reflect diverse perspectives can stimulate a more meaningful cultural dialogue.

Workshops, grants, and platforms that prioritize these values can help shift the cultural tide.

Encouraging Cross-Disciplinary Collaboration

The silos that traditionally separate disciplines are increasingly recognized as barriers to innovation. Encouraging collaboration across fields—melding the arts with sciences, technology with humanities—can lead to unprecedented creativity and solutions to complex problems. Initiatives like cross-disciplinary residencies, collaborative labs, and interdisciplinary academic programs can serve as breeding grounds for innovative ideas that have the potential to redefine cultural and societal paradigms.

Reimagining Creative Education

To sow the seeds of creativity and critical thinking in future generations, a reinvention of the educational paradigm is necessary. This entails integrating arts and cultural studies deeply within curricula, emphasizing creative problem-solving and emotional intelligence alongside traditional academic skills. Lifelong learning platforms, both online and in community settings, can ensure that individuals continue to engage with new ideas and creative practices throughout their lives, fostering a culture of continuous growth and innovation.

Leveraging Technology for Cultural Enrichment

While technology has played a role in deepening cultural stagnation, it also possesses the power to liberate and connect. The ethical use of technology—aimed at enhancing cultural participation, access, and diversity—can transform how we experience and interact with art and culture. Virtual reality art galleries, digital archives of traditional crafts, and online collaborative spaces can democratize access to culture and provide new avenues for creative expression and exploration.

Fostering Innovation and Creativity in the Age of Isolation

In an era marked by digital isolation, fostering spaces for innovation and creativity is more crucial than ever. The path forward involves creating environments that nurture connection, experimentation, and the sharing of diverse perspectives. The Rebirth of The Third Place.

Cultivating Spaces for Creative Exchange

Designing both physical and digital spaces that encourage creative exchange and collaboration is fundamental to sparking innovation. Community art centers, maker spaces, and online forums can serve as catalysts for creativity, offering platforms for creators to share their work, collaborate with others, and engage in meaningful dialogue with audiences. These spaces can act as incubators for cultural evolution, nurturing the seeds of new ideas and artistic movements.

Championing Diversity and Inclusivity

A vibrant cultural ecosystem thrives on the richness of diverse voices and perspectives. Policies and practices that promote inclusivity in the arts and media can ensure that a broad spectrum of experiences and viewpoints are represented and celebrated. Initiatives to support underrepresented artists, along with efforts to broaden the canon in education and public discourse, can enrich the cultural dialogue and foster a more empathetic and inclusive society.

Embracing Experimentation and Resilience

Innovation is inherently tied to risk, experimentation, and, inevitably, the possibility of failure. Cultivating an environment that embraces these aspects of the creative process is essential for pushing the boundaries of what is possible. Recognizing and celebrating the journey of creation, with its triumphs and challenges, can encourage artists and innovators to explore uncharted territories without fear. Awards, residencies, and community support for experimental projects can provide the necessary safety net for creative risks.

Building and Nurturing Creative Communities

The transformation from a state of cultural hibernation to a dynamic and innovative society is a collective endeavor. Establishing networks and communities that support creativity and innovation is key to this transformation. These communities can offer resources, mentorship, and collaborative opportunities, empowering creators to make meaningful contributions to the cultural landscape. Through festivals, exhibitions, and online platforms, these communities can celebrate and disseminate innovative work, inspiring further creativity and engagement.

Awakening from cultural hibernation and navigating towards a future rich in creativity and innovation requires a holistic approach that values authenticity, encourages cross-disciplinary collaboration, leverages technology thoughtfully, and fosters inclusive and supportive communities. By collectively embracing these strategies, society can rekindle the spark of creativity and chart a course towards a vibrant and dynamic cultural renaissance.

Chapter 8: The Future of Fashion and Culture

The horizon of fashion and culture, with its intertwined destinies, beckons with a blend of uncertainty and promise. This chapter embarks on a speculative journey into what the future may hold, pondering the potential trajectories of these domains under the influence of evolving societal norms, technological innovation, and a collective yearning for authenticity and sustainability.

A Sustainable Revolution in Fashion

The impending future portends a radical transformation towards sustainability in the fashion industry. This paradigm shift is anticipated to be driven by a dual approach: technological innovation and a profound change in consumer consciousness. Advances in material science promise the development of eco-friendly textiles that do not compromise on quality or aesthetics, while digital fabrication techniques like 3D printing are poised to revolutionize production processes, minimizing waste and optimizing efficiency.

Concurrently, a cultural shift towards valuing sustainability is expected to reshape consumer behavior. The rise of the conscious consumer will likely see a departure from fast fashion and a move towards a more intentional model of consumption, characterized by a preference for timeless pieces, high-quality materials, and ethical manufacturing practices. This shift could catalyze the fashion industry to embrace circular economy principles, where the lifecycle of products is extended through reuse, repair, and recycling, significantly reducing the environmental footprint.

Cultural Renaissance through Digital Means

The future of culture lies in leveraging digital technologies not as ends in themselves but as means to foster deeper human connection and creativity. The proliferation of digital platforms has the potential to democratize cultural production, offering a stage for diverse voices and stories that challenge the mainstream narrative. Virtual and augmented reality technologies could transform the way we experience art, heritage, and performance, creating immersive experiences that transcend physical and geographical limitations.

However, this digital renaissance depends on a critical balance between technology and humanity. The challenge will be to harness these tools in ways that enhance rather than replace the richness of real-world experiences and interactions. As digital and physical realms become increasingly integrated, finding innovative ways to preserve the tactile, communal, and ephemeral aspects of cultural experiences will be crucial.

Technology: A Tool for Liberation or Further Isolation?

The dual nature of technology as both liberator and isolator will become even more pronounced in the future. On one side, technology holds immense potential to break down barriers to cultural participation and expression. For instance, blockchain technology could ensure fair compensation for creators by providing transparent, tamper-proof systems for rights management and revenue distribution. Similarly, artificial intelligence and machine learning could offer personalized cultural experiences, connecting individuals with content that resonates with their unique tastes and interests.

On the flip side, the risk of technology fostering further isolation and contributing to the digital divide cannot be ignored. As cultural experiences become more digitized, ensuring equitable access to technology becomes paramount. Bridging the digital divide will require concerted efforts to provide universal access to the internet and digital literacy education, ensuring that the cultural renaissance facilitated by technology is inclusive and accessible to all.

Reimagining a Culturally Dynamic Society

The path to a culturally dynamic society is paved with the collective aspirations of a global community that values diversity, creativity, and sustainability. Envisioning this future involves imagining new forms of cultural expression that embrace the complexity and interconnectedness of our world. It calls for a culture that is fluid, continuously evolving in response to the changing tapestry of global influences and local traditions.

In this future, cultural institutions and creative industries play a pivotal role in nurturing a vibrant cultural ecosystem. This involves supporting experimental and interdisciplinary work, fostering collaborations across cultural boundaries, and providing platforms for dialogue and exchange. Education systems, too, must evolve to cultivate creative thinking, cultural empathy, and an appreciation for the arts as integral components of a well-rounded education.

Ultimately, the future of fashion and culture hinges on our collective ability to envision and create a world that reflects our highest aspirations for creativity, inclusivity, and sustainability. By embracing the challenges and opportunities of the present, we can chart a course towards a future where culture thrives as a source of connection, inspiration, and resilience.

In weaving the threads of this future, every individual, community, and institution has a role to play. Together, we can reimagine and rebuild the cultural landscape, fostering a world where fashion and culture not only reflect but also enrich the human experience, bridging divides and celebrating the diversity and dynamism of our global society.

Conclusion

As we conclude this exploration into the phenomenon of cultural hibernation and its multifaceted impacts on fashion and society, it is essential to distill the key insights gleaned from our journey and to propose a way forward. The narrative woven throughout the chapters reveals a complex tapestry of challenges and opportunities, underscoring the urgency of awakening from the slumber of cultural repetition and embracing a future marked by innovation, diversity, and sustainability.

Summary of Key Insights

The journey from the post-war era of the 1940s to the early 21st century has been characterized by seismic shifts in fashion and culture, driven by societal changes, technological advancements, and evolving aesthetic sensibilities. This historical trajectory underscores the dynamic interplay between culture and external forces, illustrating how fashion serves as both a mirror to society and a canvas for individual and collective identity.

The turn of the millennium, however, marked the onset of cultural hibernation—a period of stagnation where the rapid cycles of change gave way to the recycling of trends and a pervasive sense of ennui. Key factors contributing to this state include the saturation of the market with fast fashion, the paradoxical effects of digital connectivity leading to social isolation, and the environmental toll of unchecked consumerism.

Victor Frankl's existential philosophy, particularly his emphasis on the search for meaning, offers profound insights into overcoming the existential vacuum that parallels the contemporary cultural malaise. His ideas encourage a reevaluation of personal and collective values, advocating for a purpose-driven approach to creativity and cultural engagement.

Call to Action: Breaking Free from Cultural Hibernation

To emerge from this period of cultural hibernation, a concerted effort across multiple domains of society is required. This call to action invites individuals, communities, creators, and institutions to partake in a cultural renaissance that values authenticity, innovation, and sustainability.

1. Embrace Sustainable Practices: Transitioning away from fast fashion and disposable culture towards sustainability in all forms of cultural production and consumption is imperative. This shift demands a reevaluation of values, prioritizing long-term environmental and social well-being over immediate gratification.

2. Foster Creativity and Innovation: Cultivating environments that encourage risk-taking, interdisciplinary collaboration, and the exploration of new ideas is crucial for reinvigorating cultural dynamism. Support for the arts, education that nurtures creative thinking, and platforms that celebrate diversity and experimentation are key to this endeavor.

3. Leverage Technology Ethically: While recognizing the potential of technology to enhance or detract from the richness of cultural experience, it is vital to employ digital tools in ways that foster genuine human connection, inclusivity, and access to diverse cultural expressions.

4. Build Inclusive Communities: Strengthening the fabric of community through shared cultural experiences and dialogue can counteract the isolating effects of digital life. Creating spaces—both physical and virtual—that encourage interaction, empathy, and cultural exchange is essential for a vibrant society.

By embracing these principles, society can break free from the constraints of cultural hibernation, paving the way for a future where fashion and culture not only reflect but actively shape a world characterized by diversity, creativity, and a deep respect for the planet and its inhabitants.

Appendices

Timeline of Fashion and Cultural Changes: 1940s-2020s

This timeline encapsulates key moments in the evolution of fashion and culture over eight decades, highlighting significant trends, movements, and technological innovations that have shaped the landscape.

- 1940s: Post-war austerity and the birth of Christian Dior's "New Look"
- 1950s: Rise of consumer culture, rock 'n' roll, and the youth fashion movement
- 1960s: Cultural revolution, miniskirts, and the proliferation of counterculture styles
- 1970s: Disco, punk, and the diversification of fashion influences
- 1980s: The era of excess, power dressing, and the advent of digital technology
- 1990s: Grunge, the supermodel phenomenon, and the early days of the internet
- 2000s: The rise of fast fashion, digital social networks, and globalized culture
- 2010s-2020s: Sustainability movement, digital fashion, and the quest for authenticity

 Further Reading and Resources

- Frankl, Victor. *Man's Search for Meaning*. An essential read for understanding Frankl's existential philosophy and psychological insights.
- Fletcher, Kate. *Sustainable Fashion and Textiles: Design Journeys*. Offers a comprehensive look into sustainable practices within the fashion industry.
- Gladwell, Malcolm. *The Tipping Point: How Little Things Can Make a Big Difference*. Explores how ideas, trends, and social behaviors cross a threshold to tip into widespread popularity.

- Postrel, Virginia. *The Substance of Style: How the Rise of Aesthetic Value Is Remaking Commerce, Culture, and Consciousness*. Examines the role of aesthetics in modern culture and its implications for business and society.

These resources provide a foundation for further exploration into the themes discussed, offering insights and perspectives on the challenges and opportunities that lie ahead in fashion and culture.

Panini, Pagliacci, Prescriptions

Beyond Bread and Circuses: A Modern Quest for Meaning and Mental Wellness

Julian Del Bel

> A man goes to the doctor. He says, "Doc, I'm depressed. Life seems harsh and cruel. I feel all alone in a threatening world. What should I do?"
>
> The doctor says, "Ah, my friend, the great clown Pagliacci is in town tonight. Go and see him. He's hilarious and will surely cheer you up."

The man bursts into tears and says, "But doctor... I am Pagliacci."

Foreword

In the grand, swirling chaos that is the modern age—a circus of digital spectacles, pharmaceutical mirages, and gourmet distractions finely sliced and served on artisanal bread—it takes a peculiar kind of madness to pause and ponder the spectacle. This book, dear reader, is that madness made manifest.

What we have here is not a mere collection of observations but a roadmap through the wilderness of our collective psyche, guided by the spectral presence of Pagliacci, the clown who weeps even as he makes the world laugh. In an era where the lines between reality and performance blur more with each swipe of a screen, where our appetites are whetted with images of perfection that leave us more starved than ever, and where the promise of chemical solace is but a prescription away, this book dares to ask: What is the cost of our distractions? Are we, like the Romans before us, too entertained to notice the empire burning?

This is not your standard fare of societal critique, nor is it a detached academic treatise on the malaise of the modern man. No, this is a wild ride through the belly of the beast, a gonzo exploration of the grand illusion and the search for something genuine amidst the facades. It's a call to arms, or perhaps a call to minds, urging us to cut through the cacophony of the 21st century's grand circus to find our own truth, our own meaning amidst the bread and circuses that placate and pacify.

So buckle up, dear reader. You're not merely flipping through pages; you're embarking on a quest through the laughter and tears, the spectacle and solitude of our times. It's a journey fraught with peril and paradox, but fear not—for within this madness lies the seeds of enlightenment, and perhaps, just perhaps, a glimpse of what it means to be truly alive in the age of distraction.

Introduction to "Panini, Pagliacci, Prescriptions"

In the heart of this exploration lies a triad of symbols—Panini, Pagliacci, Prescriptions—that together weave a narrative about modern society's intricate methods of distraction, pacification, and the underlying sadness that pervades despite these efforts. The title of this book, while initially might evoke a sense of whimsical curiosity, is a meticulously chosen representation of our current socio-cultural landscape. It encapsulates the essence of how contemporary society, much like the ancient Roman concept of 'bread and circuses,' uses food (Panini), entertainment (Pagliacci), and now, prescription drugs, to maintain social order and keep the populace in a state of complacency.

"Panini, Pagliacci, Prescriptions" is not just a critique but a deep dive into the complexities of happiness, mental health, and the societal mechanisms in place that both alleviate and contribute to our collective malaise. It is an invitation to ponder on the dynamic ways in which we seek comfort, escape, and sometimes, oblivion, from the realities of our existence. Through the lens of these three seemingly disparate elements, we embark on a journey to dissect the layers of modern life's fabric, examining how far we have come and how far we still have to go in understanding the true nature of contentment and wellbeing.

The modern-day "Bread and Circuses"

The phrase 'bread and circuses' (panem et circenses) was coined by the Roman poet Juvenal, signifying the strategy of governance by which Roman leaders maintained power and control over the populace by providing the bare minimum of sustenance (bread) and ample entertainment (circuses) to distract from political disengagement and social unrest. In today's context, this concept has morphed into a more sophisticated but equally effective form of societal pacification. The 'bread' has transformed from literal sustenance into a metaphor for the endless pursuit of material comfort and culinary hedonism, exemplified by the cultural obsession with food, from gourmet paninis to exotic cuisines, signifying not just physical nourishment but a marker of status and identity.

The 'circuses,' on the other hand, have expanded beyond the physical arenas into the digital realm, where entertainment is omnipresent, accessible, and tailored to individual preferences, creating an endless loop of distraction and escapism. This digital colosseum, ranging from social media to streaming services, serves as the modern amphitheater, captivating the masses with a continuous flow of content, ensuring the audience's attention is perpetually engaged, leaving little room for critical thought or civic engagement.

Adding a third dimension to this modern-day 'bread and circuses' is the widespread use of prescription drugs as a means to manage, or sometimes mask, the psychological ramifications of living in such a society. 'Prescriptions' serve as the contemporary panacea for the maladies of the mind, offering solace in the form of chemical comfort. This triad completes the picture of a society that is at once indulged and numbed, entertained and distracted, ostensibly content yet profoundly disconnected from the roots of genuine happiness and fulfillment.

"Panini, Pagliacci, Prescriptions" explores these threads of modern life with a critical eye, aiming to uncover the layers beneath the surface of our collective pursuit of happiness. It questions the sustainability of a society built on the pillars of instant gratification, escapism, and medicated serenity, and invites readers to reflect on the true essence of joy, connection, and wellbeing in our contemporary world.

As we look into the pages that follow, let us hold a mirror to our society and ourselves, confronting the realities of our existence with openness, curiosity, and a willingness to question the status quo. The journey through "Panini, Pagliacci, Prescriptions" is more than an academic or philosophical inquiry; it is a call to awareness, a plea for mindfulness, and perhaps, a roadmap to finding more authentic and sustainable paths to happiness and fulfillment in our increasingly complex world.

Part I: Bread - From Panem to Panini

1. Historical Bread and Circuses

The Roman Origins and Its Implications for Society

The concept of "bread and circuses" originated in ancient Rome, attributed to the poet Juvenal. In his satirical commentary, he criticized the Roman populace's gradual abandonment of their historical political engagement in favor of basic food and entertainment provided by the state. This phrase, "panem et circenses," encapsulates a political strategy that has transcended centuries: the manipulation of public sentiment through the provision of basic needs and distractions to maintain social order and prevent dissent.

In Rome, this was not merely metaphorical. The state regularly distributed free grain and hosted grand spectacles, such as gladiatorial games, chariot races, and theatrical performances in the Colosseum and Circus Maximus. These entertainments served dual purposes: they kept the populace fed and amused, thus averting their attention from political matters and potential grievances against the elite, and they reinforced the power and generosity of the political leaders and the state. This approach to governance highlights a fundamental understanding of human nature—physical sustenance and sensory stimulation can significantly influence satisfaction and loyalty, often at the expense of deeper civic engagement and political activism.

Transition from Literal to Metaphorical Sustenance

The evolution from the literal interpretation of "bread" as a form of sustenance to its metaphorical significance in contemporary society reflects a shift in the methods used to placate and pacify populations. In modern contexts, "bread" transcends the basic need for food, morphing into a symbol for a wider array of material comforts and consumer goods that denote status, identity, and belonging. The modern "bread" encompasses the endless pursuit of material wealth, represented by branded luxury items, high-end culinary experiences, and the latest technological gadgets. These items serve not just as markers of personal success but as tools of distraction, keeping society focused on consumption and accumulation rather than on more substantive issues of societal welfare and political engagement.

This shift towards metaphorical sustenance is complemented by the transformation of "circuses" into forms of digital entertainment that captivate our attention and fill our leisure time, further distancing us from active participation in the civic and political arenas. The omnipresence of screens, social media, and streaming services functions as the new arena, offering a continuous stream of entertainment that keeps the populace entertained, distracted, and, significantly, placated.

The transition from literal to metaphorical sustenance has profound implications for society. It signals a deepening of the mechanisms of control and distraction, moving beyond the physical provision of food and entertainment to encompass the psychological and emotional realms. This evolution reflects a more sophisticated understanding of human desires and vulnerabilities, leveraging them to maintain social stability and discourage dissent. However, it also raises critical questions about autonomy, satisfaction, and the nature of happiness in a society increasingly oriented towards consumerism and passive entertainment.

As we look deeper into the significance of "bread" in its modern incarnations, it becomes evident that the legacy of Rome's "bread and circuses" strategy is alive and well, adapted to the nuances of contemporary life. The implications of this for individual well-being and societal health are profound, inviting a reevaluation of our values, priorities, and the meaning of true fulfillment.

2. The Gourmet Evolution: Panini as Modern Bread

Culinary Distractions in Contemporary Society

In the ever-evolving landscape of societal distractions, the culinary world has emerged as a significant player, offering not just sustenance but a form of escapism and entertainment. The transformation of bread, a fundamental element of human diet, into the gourmet panini symbolizes this shift. This evolution from basic nourishment to a culinary delight represents a broader trend where food transcends its primary function to become a source of distraction, pleasure, and even status.

The gourmet panini, with its variety of high-quality ingredients, artisan bread, and innovative combinations, is a microcosm of the culinary distractions prevalent in contemporary society. Food festivals, cooking shows, celebrity chefs, and the endless stream of food-related content on social media platforms are testament to the role of food as a cultural phenomenon that extends far beyond mere survival. This obsession with food not only satisfies the palate but also feeds the soul, providing a temporary respite from the mundanities and pressures of daily life.

These culinary distractions serve a dual purpose. On one hand, they bring joy, foster social connections, and celebrate cultural diversity through the universal language of food. On the other, they contribute to the modern-day "bread and circuses" by engaging the senses and diverting attention from pressing societal issues and personal anxieties. In a world brimming with uncertainties, the pursuit of the next gastronomic delight offers a semblance of control and a momentary escape from reality.

The Symbolism of Choice and Abundance

The gourmet panini, in its myriad forms, embodies the symbolism of choice and abundance that characterizes much of modern consumer culture. The ability to choose from a vast array of bread, cheeses, meats, vegetables, and condiments reflects a society that values variety and personalization. This abundance of choice, while seemingly beneficial, also mirrors the overwhelming nature of consumerism and the paradox of choice, where too many options can lead to dissatisfaction and indecision.

The preference for gourmet offerings over basic sustenance highlights the socio-economic disparities within society. The luxury of choice is often a privilege reserved for those with the means to afford it, exacerbating the divide between the haves and the have-nots. This dichotomy serves as a reminder of the inequalities that persist, often hidden beneath the veneer of abundance and prosperity.

The panini, therefore, is more than just a culinary delight; it is a symbol of our times, reflecting the complexities of contemporary society. It embodies the transition from survival to pleasure, from necessity to luxury, and from uniformity to diversity. Yet, it also raises questions about the sustainability of such abundance, the ethical implications of food trends, and the social responsibilities of consumers in a globalized world.

As we navigate through the gourmet evolution of modern bread, it is essential to reflect on the role of culinary distractions in our lives. While they offer moments of joy and a sense of community, they also require a mindful approach to consumption, an awareness of the broader societal implications, and a commitment to addressing the underlying issues that these distractions may serve to mask. The gourmet panini, in all its delicious complexity, serves as a delicious yet thought-provoking emblem of the times, inviting us to savor not only the flavors but also the deeper meanings it represents in our contemporary tapestry.

3. Economic and Social Implications

How Consumerism Feeds Into the Distraction

In the intricate dance of modern society, consumerism plays a pivotal role, not merely as an economic engine but as a profound source of distraction. This phenomenon, deeply intertwined with the fabric of daily life, extends far beyond the accumulation of goods, infiltrating every aspect of our existence from what we eat to how we entertain ourselves. The gourmet panini, emblematic of a society that revels in the luxury of choice and abundance, serves as a perfect illustration of how consumerism has evolved into a sophisticated form of the ancient "bread and circuses," keeping the populace engaged, entertained, and ostensibly content.

Consumerism, in its modern guise, is not just about satisfying basic needs or desires but about constructing identities, signaling status, and fostering a sense of belonging. The act of consumption becomes a means of distraction, a way to momentarily escape the realities and pressures of life. This distraction is layered, offering not just temporary relief from boredom or stress but also a diversion from more substantive societal issues and personal existential queries. It encourages a focus on the superficial and the immediate, often at the expense of deeper engagement with the world around us.

The constant bombardment of advertising and the pervasive presence of social media platforms have intensified this distraction, creating a cycle of desire and fulfillment that is ever-hard to break. The quest for the next purchase, the latest gastronomic trend, or the newest gadget consumes considerable mental bandwidth, diverting attention from civic duties, community engagement, and the pursuit of personal growth.

The Gap Between Luxury and Necessity

The distinction between luxury and necessity, increasingly blurred in the age of consumerism, has profound economic and social implications. The gourmet panini, a luxury iteration of a basic food item, symbolizes this shift, where what was once considered a simple meal has been elevated to a status symbol, a marker of taste and economic capability. This elevation of the mundane into the realm of luxury highlights the growing gap between those who can indulge in such choices and those for whom basic necessities remain a struggle.

This gap is not merely a matter of economic inequality but a reflection of deeper social divisions. The ability to participate in the consumer culture, to indulge in the distractions it offers, becomes a marker of social inclusion. Meanwhile, those unable to afford these luxuries find themselves marginalized, not just economically but culturally and socially. This division compounds feelings of alienation and disenfranchisement among the less affluent, undermining social cohesion and fostering an environment ripe for discontent and division.

The emphasis on luxury consumption underscores a societal value system that prioritizes material success and external appearances over more substantive achievements and qualities. This shift has implications for the collective psyche, promoting a sense of dissatisfaction and perpetual longing, as the goalposts of success and happiness continually move. It also raises questions about sustainability, as the relentless pursuit of luxury and novelty fuels patterns of consumption that strain the planet's resources and enflame environmental degradation.

As we witness the economic and social implications of consumerism, it becomes increasingly clear that the distractions it offers, while comforting in the short term, carry significant long-term costs. Bridging the gap between luxury and necessity requires a concerted effort to foster a more inclusive society, one that values and supports the well-being of all its members. It also necessitates a reevaluation of our collective priorities, encouraging a shift towards more sustainable and fulfilling modes of living that transcend the endless cycle of desire and consumption. In this context, the gourmet panini, delicious though it may be, serves as a poignant reminder of the complexities and contradictions of our contemporary world, urging us to seek deeper, more meaningful forms of sustenance and satisfaction.

Part II: Circuses - Entertainment and Escapism

4. Digital Colosseums

The modern iteration of circuses has transcended the physical realms of entertainment to manifest into the digital world, creating what can aptly be described as "Digital Colosseums." These platforms encompass the vast array of digital and virtual entertainment that captures and sustains public attention in the contemporary era. Through an exploration of the role of media and technology in modern entertainment and the burgeoning presence of virtual realities, we look into how these digital colosseums serve as the ultimate distraction, mirroring the societal function of their ancient Roman counterparts.

The Role of Media and Technology in Modern Entertainment

Media and technology have fundamentally transformed the landscape of entertainment, ushering in an era where access to amusement is limitless, instantaneous, and pervasively integrated into daily life. The evolution of digital technology, especially the internet, smartphones, and streaming services, has created an unceasing flow of content, making entertainment accessible with a mere click. This shift has not only changed how entertainment is consumed but has also altered the nature of what is considered entertaining, expanding it to include everything from blockbuster movies and binge-worthy series to video games, social media feeds, and virtual reality experiences.

The digital colosseum is marked by its ability to engage audiences in a multidimensional entertainment experience, blurring the lines between passive viewership and active participation. Social media platforms, for example, have become arenas where entertainment is both consumed and produced, with users playing the roles of spectator, creator, and critic simultaneously. This participatory aspect of digital entertainment enhances its allure, making it a more potent form of distraction that is tailored to individual preferences and interests.

Virtual Realities as the Ultimate Distraction

Among the spectacles of the digital colosseum, virtual reality (VR) stands out as the ultimate form of escapism. By immersing users in entirely constructed environments, VR offers an escape from the mundane or stressful aspects of real life into worlds limited only by imagination. These virtual realities provide not just entertainment but an experiential diversion that can feel more real than reality itself, offering unprecedented levels of engagement and immersion.

Virtual realities go beyond traditional forms of entertainment by enabling individuals to live out fantasies, explore unreachable destinations, and experience impossible scenarios without leaving their homes. This capacity for immersive distraction raises both possibilities and concerns. On one hand, VR has significant potential for education, therapy, and social connection, offering immersive experiences that can promote empathy, learning, and healing. On the other hand, the seductive allure of these virtual worlds poses risks of addiction, disengagement from actual societal issues, and a blurring of the lines between reality and simulation.

The digital colosseum, with virtual realities as its most captivating spectacle, embodies the modern-day "bread and circuses," providing an ever-expanding universe of entertainment that captivates the global audience. This digital escapism serves a function similar to that of the ancient circuses, offering relief and diversion from the pressures of contemporary life. However, it also prompts critical questions about the impact of such distractions on individual well-being, social engagement, and the collective capacity to address real-world challenges.

As we weave through the complexities of the digital age, the role of these digital colosseums in shaping society, culture, and individual psychology continues to evolve. The balance between harnessing the benefits of these platforms for positive ends and mitigating their potential for distraction and disengagement is a central challenge of our time, prompting ongoing reflection and dialogue about the place of entertainment in a balanced, fulfilling life.

5. Celebrity Culture and Spectacle

How Celebrities Have Become the Modern Gladiators

In the grand arena of modern entertainment, celebrities have ascended to a status reminiscent of the ancient gladiators, captivating the masses with their talents, lives, and even their downfalls. This transformation is not merely a product of their abilities or the public's fascination with talent but a sophisticated orchestration of media, technology, and a culture that thrives on spectacle. Just as gladiators were celebrated and idolized in ancient Rome, drawing the populace to the Colosseum, today's celebrities draw crowds to screens of all sizes, from smartphones to cinemas, becoming the centerpiece of the digital colosseums.

The mechanisms behind this phenomenon are well structured. The pervasive reach of social media platforms, reality TV, and 24/7 celebrity news cycles create an omnipresent entertainment spectacle, where celebrities are both performers and products, constantly under the spotlight. Their lives, curated or candid, are dissected and devoured by the public, creating a constant stream of content that feeds the modern appetite for distraction and escapism. This relentless exposure not only elevates celebrities to a status akin to modern-day demigods but also intertwines their personas with the identity and aspirations of the masses.

The Impact of Idolatry on Societal Values

The idolization of celebrities has profound implications for societal values, shaping norms, behaviors, and aspirations in both conspicuous and subtle ways. This phenomenon promotes a culture of emulation, where the lifestyles, choices, and even the controversies surrounding celebrities become benchmarks for success, beauty, and worthiness. The glamour and opulence associated with celebrity lifestyles set unrealistic standards, fostering a culture of dissatisfaction and perpetual striving among the masses. It propagates the notion that visibility, wealth, and external validation are paramount, often at the expense of virtues like authenticity, community, and personal fulfillment.

Moreover, celebrity culture has contributed to the commodification of privacy and the blurring of lines between public and personal spheres. The spectacle of celebrity lives creates an appetite for constant entertainment that infringes on the private, sometimes leading to invasive scrutiny and a pervasive paparazzi culture. This spectacle diminishes the value placed on privacy, intimacy, and genuine human connections, replacing them with a voyeuristic consumption of curated personas.

The idolatry of celebrities also influences societal values through the phenomenon of "celebrity activism." While the involvement of celebrities in social and political causes can have positive impacts, bringing attention and resources to important issues, it also raises questions about the depth and authenticity of such engagements. The celebrity endorsement of causes can simplify complex issues into digestible narratives, overshadowing nuanced discussions and grassroots movements. It reflects and reinforces a culture that values the symbolic over the substantive, where gesture often supersedes genuine action.

The ascendancy of celebrities as the modern gladiators in the digital colosseums of our time serves as a powerful form of entertainment and escapism. However, it also mirrors and molds societal values in ways that merit critical examination. The spectacle of celebrity culture, while providing diversion and delight, prompts a reflection on the deeper values and aspirations that define us as individuals and as a society. It invites a reconsideration of what we idolize, aspire to, and how we navigate the fine line between admiration and idolatry in a world awash with spectacle.

6. Sports and Spectacles

Athletic Endeavors as Communal Opiates

The realm of sports, transcending mere physical contests, has emerged as a vital cog in the machinery of modern entertainment and societal pacification. These athletic spectacles, akin to the communal opiates of the masses, offer not just diversion but a profound sense of belonging and identity to diverse communities around the globe. This phenomenon, deeply ingrained in human culture, leverages the universal appeal of physical prowess and competition, transforming sports into a global language of unity and rivalry.

The power of sports as communal opiates lies in their ability to congregate individuals from disparate backgrounds, creating a shared experience that momentarily transcends societal divisions. This unifying force, potent and pervasive, fosters a collective consciousness that is both escapist and euphoric. The emotional investment in teams and athletes provides a sense of purpose and belonging, filling voids and mitigating the existential ennui that pervades modern life. Moreover, these athletic endeavors, with their inherent drama, triumphs, and defeats, offer a narrative richness that mirrors the complexities of human life, providing a cathartic outlet for the vicissitudes of the human experience.

The Economics of Sports as a Distraction Mechanism

The intricate relationship between sports and economics is a testament to the role of athletic spectacles as a sophisticated distraction mechanism. The sports industry, encompassing broadcasting rights, merchandise, ticket sales, and sponsorships, is a multibillion-dollar global enterprise that capitalizes on the universal appeal of athletic competition. This economic behemoth not only fuels the global entertainment apparatus but also serves as a pivotal distraction mechanism, directing public attention and financial resources towards spectacle and away from pressing societal issues.

The commodification of sports has profound implications for its role as a societal opiate. The saturation of media with sports content, the commercialization of athletes as brand ambassadors, and the relentless pursuit of profit have elevated sports to a paramount position in the hierarchy of distractions. This economic model reinforces the consumerist ethos, encouraging a cycle of consumption and emotional investment that keeps the masses engaged and diverted. The economics of sports, thus, is not merely a matter of financial transactions but a complex system that perpetuates the distraction of the populace, maintaining social order by channeling collective energies into the vicarious participation in athletic endeavors.

The economics of sports also highlights the disparity between the opulence of the industry and the broader societal needs. The allocation of substantial resources to sports infrastructure, events, and salaries, in contrast to underfunded public services and social programs, raises ethical and economic questions. This discrepancy underscores the prioritization of entertainment and distraction over the welfare and development of society, reflecting broader themes of inequality and misallocation of resources.

Sports, as modern spectacles, serve a dual role as communal opiates and economic engines, offering a potent mix of diversion, unity, and commercialism. This dual role underscores the complex interplay between entertainment, economics, and societal pacification. As athletic spectacles continue to captivate the global imagination, their impact on social cohesion, economic disparities, and the collective focus of society warrants a deeper understanding and critical reflection, challenging us to contemplate the true cost and value of our communal opiates.

7. The Rise of Prescription Culture

Historical Context of Drug Use for Social Pacification

The use of substances to alter consciousness or mood is a practice as ancient as humanity itself, serving various purposes across different cultures and epochs. However, the conceptual framework of using drugs specifically for social pacification has a varied history, intertwined with the evolution of medicine, societal norms, and governance. In ancient times, substances like opium were used not only for their analgesic properties but also to sedate the masses during periods of unrest or discontent. This dual use underscores a recurring theme throughout history: the governance of populations through the modulation of mood and consciousness.

The transition to what we recognize today as a prescription culture began in earnest in the late 19th and early 20th centuries, paralleling the rise of modern pharmaceutical science and the establishment of the medical profession's authority. This era marked the beginning of the systematic study, production, and regulation of drugs for a wide array of psychological and physical conditions. It was also a period that saw the burgeoning of the concept of mental health as a crucial component of overall well-being, leading to increased attention to and treatment of mental and emotional disorders with pharmaceuticals.

The Pharmaceutical Industry's Role in Modern Society

In contemporary society, the pharmaceutical industry has ascended to a position of unprecedented influence, shaping not only health care practices but also societal attitudes towards health, wellness, and illness. This industry's role is complex and integrated, driving innovation and providing treatments for countless conditions while also engendering a culture where medication is often seen as the first recourse for a broad spectrum of life's challenges.

The rise of prescription culture in modern society can be attributed, in part, to the pharmaceutical industry's mastery of marketing, lobbying, and the framing of health issues. Through direct-to-consumer advertising, a practice allowed in only a few countries, the industry has been able to influence public perception and demand for medications directly. This marketing is not just about promoting specific drugs but also about medicalizing various aspects of human experience, suggesting pharmaceutical solutions for a range of problems that might once have been considered part of the normal spectrum of life's ups and downs.

The industry's role extends into the political and regulatory realms, where lobbying efforts and financial contributions can influence policy and drug approval processes. This influence can sometimes lead to broader prescription practices and a more medication-centric approach to health and wellness, contributing to the normalization of drug use for social, emotional, and psychological management.

The emergence of prescription culture reflects a significant shift in how society approaches well-being, with increasing reliance on pharmaceutical solutions to navigate life's complexities. While this shift has undeniably brought relief and improved quality of life for many, it also raises critical questions about the implications of such dependency on drugs for individual autonomy, the nature of health and illness, and the broader socio-economic impacts of pharmaceuticalizing human experience.

The pharmaceutical industry's central role in modern society is a testament to its success in advancing medical science and improving lives. Yet, it also highlights the need for a balanced approach to health that considers the holistic aspects of well-being, including social, environmental, and lifestyle factors, alongside pharmaceutical interventions. As prescription culture continues to evolve, it invites a deeper examination of the ways in which society addresses health and happiness, urging a reevaluation of our collective reliance on pharmacological solutions to the challenges of human existence.

8. Mental Health and Medication

The Fine Line Between Treatment and Dependency

The relationship between mental health treatment and medication is intricate, characterized by the delicate balance between therapeutic benefit and the risk of dependency. This balance is central to contemporary mental health care, reflecting a nuanced understanding of mental health disorders as complex interplays of biological, psychological, and social factors.

Medications, particularly psychotropic drugs, have revolutionized the treatment of many mental health conditions, offering relief from symptoms for countless individuals and enabling them to lead fuller, more productive lives. However, the success of these medications has also ushered in challenges, notably the potential for dependency and the societal implications it entails.

Dependency on mental health medications can manifest in various forms, from physiological reliance to the psychological belief that medication alone is sufficient for wellness. This situation is compounded by the nature of mental health disorders, which often require long-term management. The distinction between using medication as a necessary tool for treatment and developing a dependency that overshadows other aspects of care is nuanced. It requires careful consideration of individual patient needs, continuous monitoring, and, ideally, an integrated treatment plan that encompasses both pharmacological and non-pharmacological interventions.

The conversation around dependency is not just clinical but deeply personal, touching on themes of identity, autonomy, and the desire for a "normal" life free from the constraints of medication. It raises ethical questions about the responsibility of healthcare providers, the pharmaceutical industry, and society at large in supporting individuals' mental health journeys without inadvertently fostering dependency.

The Debate over Medication vs. Holistic Approaches

The discourse on mental health treatment has increasingly highlighted a debate between medication-based approaches and holistic or alternative therapies. This debate reflects broader philosophical questions about the nature of health and wellness, the role of medicine in society, and the values that guide mental health care practices.

Proponents of medication emphasize the importance of addressing the biological aspects of mental health disorders, citing the efficacy of pharmacological interventions in managing symptoms and improving quality of life. For many conditions, such as severe depression, bipolar disorder, and schizophrenia, medications are an essential component of treatment, often necessary for stabilization and function.

Conversely, advocates for holistic approaches argue for the inclusion of lifestyle factors, psychotherapy, and alternative treatments in managing mental health. They highlight the importance of addressing the root causes of mental distress, such as trauma, lifestyle, and environmental factors, rather than solely treating symptoms. Holistic approaches often encompass a wide range of therapies, including cognitive-behavioral therapy, mindfulness practices, dietary changes, and exercise, among others.

The debate between medication and holistic approaches is not necessarily an either/or proposition but rather a call for a more integrated and personalized approach to mental health care. An increasing number of mental health professionals advocate for a model that combines the best of both worlds, recognizing that medication can be crucial for some individuals while others might benefit more from alternative therapies. The goal is to develop a nuanced, patient-centered approach that empowers individuals to manage their mental health in a way that aligns with their values, preferences, and the complexity of their conditions.

This conversation underscores the evolving nature of mental health care, encouraging ongoing dialogue, research, and innovation to better meet the diverse needs of individuals dealing with mental health challenges. It invites society to rethink mental health treatment, advocating for a more compassionate, holistic, and personalized approach that respects the dignity and autonomy of those seeking to improve their mental well-being.

9. Societal Impact of Prescription Dependency

How Widespread Prescription Drug Use Affects Community Dynamics

The fabric of communities is intricately woven with the threads of individual and collective health, well-being, and resilience. The widespread use of prescription drugs, particularly those with high dependency and addiction potential, introduces complex dynamics into this fabric, affecting not just individuals but the entire community. This impact manifests in various ways, from altering interpersonal relationships to influencing the broader socio-economic landscape.

One of the primary ways in which widespread prescription drug use affects community dynamics is through the alteration of social roles and interactions. Dependency can lead to increased isolation of individuals, as the focus on obtaining and using medications takes precedence over social engagements and responsibilities. This isolation can weaken community bonds and reduce the cohesiveness necessary for collective action and support. Moreover, families often bear the brunt of the consequences of prescription drug dependency, facing challenges ranging from financial strain to emotional distress.

The ripple effects of widespread prescription drug use extend to the workforce, where dependency can result in decreased productivity, higher absenteeism, and increased healthcare costs. These economic pressures can strain public and private resources, diverting funds from other community needs and initiatives. Furthermore, communities with high rates of prescription drug dependency may also see shifts in crime rates and public safety concerns, as the demand for these drugs can fuel illegal markets and related criminal activity.

The Consequences of a Medicated Populace

The societal impact of a medicated populace is dynamic, touching on economic, social, and ethical dimensions. Economically, the direct and indirect costs of widespread prescription drug use are significant. Healthcare systems face the burden of treating not only the side effects and complications of long-term medication use but also the conditions related to dependency and withdrawal. These challenges are compounded by the costs associated with lost productivity and the need for rehabilitation services.

Socially, the consequences of a medicated populace are profound. Dependency can erode the sense of community and mutual support, as individuals struggling with addiction are often stigmatized, further marginalizing them and making recovery more challenging. The normalization of prescription drug use for a broad range of conditions also shifts societal attitudes toward health and wellness, potentially undervaluing the benefits of non-pharmacological interventions and preventive measures.

Ethically, the widespread use of prescription drugs raises questions about the responsibility of various stakeholders, including the pharmaceutical industry, healthcare providers, and policymakers. The balance between providing necessary medical treatment and preventing over-medication and dependency is delicate and complex. It requires vigilant regulation, ethical marketing practices, and informed, patient-centered care. Moreover, there is a growing call for societal structures that prioritize mental health and wellness, offering support systems that go beyond medication.

The societal impact of prescription dependency underscores the need for a holistic approach to health and well-being, one that encompasses not only medical interventions but also addresses the social determinants of health. Strengthening community ties, offering comprehensive support systems, and fostering environments that promote physical and mental health can mitigate the consequences of a medicated populace. As communities grapple with these challenges, the conversation around prescription drug use, dependency, and health care priorities continues to evolve, highlighting the importance of collective action, empathy, and resilience in navigating the complexities of modern health and wellness.

10. The Pagliacci Paradox

Exploring the Joke and Its Relevance to Mental Health Awareness

The Pagliacci joke, often recounted in discussions on irony and tragedy, speaks of a man who visits a doctor, overwhelmed by sadness and seeking relief. The doctor advises him to see the great clown Pagliacci to find joy. The man, tearfully, reveals he is Pagliacci. This anecdote, simple yet profound, encapsulates the paradox of outward appearances versus inner realities, particularly in the context of mental health. It serves as a poignant reminder that the facade of happiness or normalcy can mask deep suffering and that mental anguish knows no bounds, affecting individuals regardless of their public persona or profession.

The relevance of the Pagliacci joke to mental health awareness lies in its stark illumination of the complexities of human emotion and the often invisible nature of psychological pain. It challenges the societal stigma around mental health, urging a deeper understanding and empathy for those who, like Pagliacci, smile in the light yet struggle in the shadows. The joke invites society to reconsider its perceptions of happiness and success and to acknowledge that mental health issues can afflict anyone, irrespective of their external achievements or appearances.

This narrative has gained traction in modern discourse on mental health, serving as a powerful metaphor for the importance of looking beyond the surface. It emphasizes the need for open conversations about mental health, the dismantling of stigma, and the critical importance of providing support and resources for those grappling with mental health challenges. In a world where the pressure to maintain a facade of perfection is pervasive, the Pagliacci paradox stands as a call to action, advocating for authenticity, compassion, and a more profound commitment to understanding and addressing mental health issues

The Clown as a Symbol of Hidden Sorrow

The figure of the clown, traditionally seen as an embodiment of joy and entertainment, acquires a deeper, more nuanced significance in the context of the Pagliacci paradox. In this narrative, the clown becomes a symbol of the dichotomy between public perception and private reality, embodying the concealment of pain behind a mask of happiness. This symbolism speaks to the broader human experience of masking one's true feelings, whether due to societal pressures, fear of judgment, or the internalization of stigma associated with sadness or vulnerability.

The clown's painted smile and performative gaiety, juxtaposed with hidden sorrow, mirror the societal expectation to present a polished, untroubled exterior. This expectation can hinder individuals from seeking help or expressing their struggles, exacerbating feelings of isolation and despair. The clown, therefore, becomes a poignant metaphor for the silent battle many face, highlighting the courage it takes to reveal one's vulnerabilities and the critical need for a supportive and understanding community.

The symbolism of the clown in the Pagliacci paradox encourages a reevaluation of the ways society engages with entertainment and those who provide it. It prompts reflection on the humanity of entertainers, artists, and public figures, reminding audiences of the complexity of human emotion that lies behind the facade of any performance. This awareness fosters a deeper connection and empathy, encouraging a more compassionate and inclusive approach to mental health.

The Pagliacci paradox, with its compelling narrative and symbolic imagery, serves as a vital touchstone in the discourse on mental health awareness. It challenges societal norms and perceptions, advocating for a more nuanced understanding of happiness, success, and the universal nature of psychological struggle. By embracing the lessons of this paradox, society can move toward a more empathetic and supportive approach to mental health, where the masks can be lowered, and genuine healing can begin.

11. Depression in the Spotlight

The Prevalence of Depression in the Age of Information

In an era defined by unprecedented access to information and connectivity, the shadow of depression looms large, casting a stark contrast to the brightly lit screens that promise endless knowledge and social engagement. The age of information, while offering myriad benefits, has also facilitated a unique set of challenges and stressors that contribute to the rising prevalence of depression. This phenomenon is characterized by a constant bombardment of news, the pressures of social media perfectionism, and the paradoxical isolation felt in a hyper-connected world. These factors, combined with the traditional stressors of modern life, have contributed to an environment where depression not only thrives but is also more visible than ever before.

The visibility of depression in the information age is a double-edged sword. On one hand, it has led to increased awareness and destigmatization of mental health issues, encouraging conversations that were once taboo and pushing mental health to the forefront of public discourse. On the other hand, the sheer volume of information and the tendency towards sensationalism can overwhelm individuals, exacerbating feelings of inadequacy, anxiety, and loneliness. Furthermore, the comparison culture fostered by social media platforms often presents a skewed reality that glamorizes success and happiness, leaving little room for the acknowledgment of struggle and pain, thereby deepening the chasm of isolation felt by those battling depression.

Public Figures and the Illusion of Happiness

The role of public figures in shaping perceptions of happiness and success has never been more significant. Celebrities, influencers, and other public personas often project an image of perfect lives filled with happiness, wealth, and success, a portrayal that can distort public expectations of what happiness should look like. This illusion, meticulously crafted and curated for public consumption, stands in stark contrast to the reality of human experience, which encompasses a spectrum of emotions, including periods of struggle and despair.

The impact of this illusion on societal attitudes towards depression is profound. It perpetuates the myth that happiness is a constant state of being, achievable through success and material wealth, and that any deviation from this state is abnormal or a failure. This narrative can make individuals reluctant to admit their struggles, fearing judgment or perceived inadequacy. Moreover, when public figures themselves confront depression, it often comes as a shock to the public, challenging the very illusions they helped propagate. These moments can serve as powerful catalysts for change, offering opportunities to dispel myths about depression, highlight the universality of mental health struggles, and foster a more authentic and compassionate dialogue around mental well-being.

However, the spotlight on depression, particularly when it involves public figures, must be navigated with care and responsibility. Sensationalizing or trivializing their experiences can do more harm than good, underscoring the need for respectful and informed discussion that emphasizes empathy, understanding, and the complex nature of mental health. By addressing the illusion of happiness and acknowledging the full spectrum of human emotion, society can move towards a more nuanced and realistic understanding of well-being, one that embraces vulnerability and supports individuals in their journey towards mental health.

Depression in the age of information presents unique challenges and opportunities for societal growth and understanding. By dismantling the illusions of happiness perpetuated by public figures and confronting the realities of depression with compassion and openness, we can foster a culture that values mental health, encourages authentic expression, and supports individuals through their darkest times. This shift requires a collective effort to redefine success and happiness in more inclusive, realistic terms, paving the way for a healthier, more connected society.

12. The Role of Humor and Tragedy

Coping Mechanisms in Confronting Societal Malaise

In the complex tapestry of human experience, humor and tragedy are threads that run deep, reflecting the duality of our existence. These elements serve not only as reflections of societal malaise but also as coping mechanisms, offering solace and understanding in times of distress. This duality encapsulates the ability of individuals and societies to find laughter in sorrow and meaning in suffering, illustrating the resilience of the human spirit.

Humor, with its capacity to bring lightness to darkness, acts as a critical coping mechanism in confronting societal challenges. It allows individuals to create distance from their troubles, if only momentarily, offering a different perspective and a way to process difficult emotions. Moreover, humor can serve as a form of social commentary, highlighting the absurdities of certain societal norms and behaviors, thereby fostering a collective sense of recognition and camaraderie among those who share in the jest. This communal laughter becomes a unifying force, breaking down barriers and creating a shared space for dialogue and understanding.

Tragedy, on the other hand, confronts us with the depth of human suffering and vulnerability. It forces a reckoning with the realities of pain, loss, and despair, challenging individuals and societies to find meaning amidst suffering. Tragedy, in its portrayal of the human condition, encourages empathy, reflection, and a deeper connection to the collective human experience. It reminds us of our shared vulnerabilities, promoting a sense of solidarity and compassion.

The Therapeutic Value of Laughter and the Arts

The therapeutic value of laughter, often hailed as the best medicine, lies in its immediate and palpable effects on both the mind and body. Laughter triggers the release of endorphins, the body's natural feel-good chemicals, promoting an overall sense of well-being and temporarily relieving pain. It also reduces the level of stress hormones, helping to mitigate the effects of stress, anxiety, and depression. Beyond its physiological benefits, laughter fosters social connections, strengthens relationships, and enhances emotional resilience, making it a powerful antidote to the isolation and alienation that often accompany societal malaise.

The arts, encompassing a broad spectrum of human creative expression, from literature and painting to theater and music, serve as a profound source of therapeutic value. They offer avenues for expression, reflection, and catharsis, allowing individuals to process and articulate their experiences, emotions, and innermost thoughts. The arts can challenge perceptions, provoke thought, and inspire change, facilitating personal growth and healing. Moreover, engaging with the arts, whether as creators or observers, provides a sense of purpose and belonging, connecting individuals to the larger human narrative and offering solace in the shared experience of life's beauty and tragedy.

The interplay of humor and tragedy in coping with societal malaise underscores the complexity of human resilience and the nuanced nature of healing. These mechanisms, through their capacity to elicit laughter and provoke reflection, not only provide immediate relief from distress but also foster long-term emotional and psychological growth. By embracing the therapeutic value of laughter and the arts, individuals and societies can navigate the challenges of existence with grace, forging connections, finding meaning, and celebrating the richness of the human experience in all its shades.

13. Mindful Consumption

Strategies for Individual and Collective Awareness

In a world inundated with endless streams of information, products, and entertainment, mindful consumption emerges as a vital practice for fostering individual and collective well-being. It involves the conscious engagement with the material and digital worlds, encouraging a thoughtful approach to what we consume, how we consume it, and the impact of our consumption habits on our lives and society at large. Mindful consumption is not merely about restraint but about cultivating awareness, appreciation, and a sense of responsibility towards the broader consequences of our choices.

For Individuals:

1. Intentionality in Consumption: Begin by evaluating the motivations behind consumption. Whether it's physical goods, digital content, or social media, ask yourself if it serves a genuine need or interest, or if it's driven by impulse, social pressure, or an attempt to fill an emotional void.

2. Digital Detox: Regularly schedule periods where you disconnect from digital devices and platforms. This practice helps reduce information overload, fosters mental clarity, and encourages engagement with the physical world and real-life relationships.

3. Cultivate Mindfulness Practices: Engage in activities that enhance focus and presence, such as meditation, yoga, or journaling.

Mindfulness practices aid in developing self-awareness and the ability to make more deliberate choices about consumption.

4. Educate Yourself: Understand the ethical, environmental, and social impacts of your consumption habits. This knowledge can motivate more sustainable and ethical choices, aligning personal values with actions.

For Collectives:

1. Community Engagement: Participate in or create forums for discussing and sharing strategies on mindful consumption. Communities can foster support systems that encourage more conscious lifestyles.

2. Promote Ethical and Sustainable Choices: Through collective action, communities can support businesses and initiatives that prioritize ethical production, sustainability, and social responsibility, influencing market trends and corporate practices.

3. Advocate for Transparency: Demand greater transparency from companies regarding their products' lifecycle, including sourcing, production, and disposal processes. This awareness can drive more informed consumer decisions at a collective level.

Balancing Distraction, Entertainment, and Fulfillment

The challenge in today's society lies in balancing the allure of distraction and entertainment with the pursuit of genuine fulfillment. Distractions, while offering temporary relief and enjoyment, often lead to a cycle of short-lived satisfaction and subsequent emptiness. True fulfillment, conversely, is derived from engagement in activities that provide meaning, growth, and a sense of accomplishment.

1. Prioritize Meaningful Engagement: Identify activities and pursuits that provide a sense of purpose and joy beyond passive

consumption. This could involve creative hobbies, learning new skills, or engaging in volunteer work.

2. Set Boundaries: Establish clear boundaries for engaging with digital platforms and entertainment. Limiting time spent on such activities can free up time for more fulfilling pursuits.

3. Cultivate Deep Connections: Invest in relationships that provide depth and meaning. Authentic connections with others offer emotional fulfillment that cannot be matched by superficial entertainment.

4. Embrace Boredom: View boredom as an opportunity for creativity and reflection rather than a state to be avoided. Boredom can serve as a catalyst for exploring new interests and ideas.

Mindful consumption, both as an individual practice and a collective endeavor, offers a path towards a more balanced, fulfilling life. By choosing intentionality over impulse, and meaningful engagement over mere distraction, individuals and societies can navigate towards a future marked by greater awareness, sustainability, and well-being.

14. Mental Health Advocacy and Support

The Importance of Accessible Mental Health Resources

Accessible mental health resources are fundamental to the well-being of individuals and the health of communities at large. The ability to obtain professional help, support services, and information about mental health should not be considered a luxury but a basic human right. Accessibility in this context goes beyond physical availability; it encompasses affordability, cultural sensitivity, and the elimination of barriers to entry, ensuring that everyone, regardless of their background or socioeconomic status, can receive the help they need.

Creating Pathways to Treatment: Ensuring that individuals can find and receive care without undue hardship is crucial. This includes streamlining the process of seeking help, from initial consultations to ongoing treatment, and providing a variety of treatment modalities to suit different needs and preferences.

Integration of Mental Health into Primary Care: By integrating mental health services into primary healthcare settings, we can detect and treat mental health issues earlier, making care more accessible and less stigmatized.

Digital and Community Resources: The expansion of telehealth services, online support groups, and community-based programs can significantly improve access to mental health resources, especially in underserved or remote areas.

Education and Training: Increasing the number of trained mental health professionals and offering continuous education on the latest treatments and approaches are vital steps toward improving service accessibility.

Breaking the Stigma Surrounding Mental Illness and Treatment

Stigma is one of the most significant barriers to seeking help for mental health issues. It manifests through societal attitudes, media portrayals, and even the language we use to talk about mental health, often leading to shame, discrimination, and isolation for those affected.

Open Conversations: Encouraging open, honest discussions about mental health in families, schools, workplaces, and public forums can demystify mental illness and dispel myths, making it easier for individuals to seek help without fear of judgment.

Role of Media and Influencers: Media outlets and public figures have a powerful role in shaping perceptions. Responsible reporting on mental health issues, along with influencers sharing their own experiences, can have a profound impact on public attitudes, fostering a more compassionate and informed society.

Education and Awareness Campaigns: Educational initiatives that focus on the realities of mental health conditions, the effectiveness of treatment, and the strength it takes to seek help can change societal views and empower individuals to support themselves and others.

Supportive Policies and Practices: Implementing policies that protect the rights of individuals with mental health conditions and promote mental wellness in all areas of society, including the workplace, educational institutions, and within the healthcare system, is essential for breaking down stigma.

Peer Support and Advocacy: Peer support groups and advocacy organizations play a crucial role in breaking the stigma, providing a platform for shared experiences, mutual support, and collective action towards systemic change.

Mental health advocacy and support are not just about providing resources but about creating an environment where seeking help is seen as a sign of strength, not a weakness. By making mental health resources accessible and working tirelessly to break the stigma surrounding mental illness and treatment, we can build a society that supports the mental well-being of all its members. This approach not only aids in the recovery of those directly affected but also enriches the social fabric, fostering a community characterized by empathy, understanding, and resilience.

Epilogue

Reflecting on the Journey from Distraction to Awareness

As we conclude our exploration of "Panini, Pagliacci, Prescriptions," we find ourselves at a juncture of reflection and anticipation. This journey, from the grasp of modern-day distractions to a heightened state of awareness, has unfolded a tapestry rich with insights into the human condition and the societal constructs that shape our lives. We've navigated the realms of indulgence, entertainment, and medicated ease, only to uncover the deeper currents of longing, despair, and the quest for meaning that flow beneath.

The journey has been one of contrasts—between the ephemeral satisfaction offered by the world's paninis and circuses and the enduring fulfillment that comes from confronting and understanding our own Pagliacci. It has highlighted the complexity of our pursuit of happiness in an age where the answers seem just a click away, yet genuine contentment remains elusive. This exploration has served not only as a critique of contemporary society's predilections for distraction and avoidance but also as a mirror reflecting our own vulnerabilities and capacities for resilience.

The Path Forward for Society

The path forward for society, illuminated by the insights garnered through our exploration, calls for a collective awakening—a shift from passive consumption to active engagement, from distraction to presence, from isolation to connection. It is a path that demands mindfulness in our interactions with the world and compassion in our responses to one another's struggles. This journey towards a more aware, more compassionate society begins with individual choices but finds its strength in collective action.

Cultivating Mindfulness and Empathy: By fostering mindfulness, we learn to navigate the deluge of information and stimuli with discernment, choosing paths that lead to growth and connection. Empathy, strengthened through our shared vulnerabilities, becomes the bridge that connects our individual experiences, fostering a society that values support over judgment, understanding over indifference.

Prioritizing Mental Health and Holistic Well-being: Recognizing the integral role of mental health in overall well-being, society must prioritize accessible, comprehensive care that respects the diversity of human experiences. Breaking down the barriers of stigma and embracing a holistic approach to health can transform our communal landscape into one where healing and support flourish.

Reimagining Success and Fulfillment: The journey from distraction to awareness invites a reevaluation of societal definitions of success and happiness. By valuing experiences that nourish the soul over those that merely entertain, and by prioritizing relationships and personal growth over material gains, we can redefine success in terms that foster genuine fulfillment.

Embracing the Arts and Creativity: The arts, in their myriad forms, offer powerful avenues for expression, connection, and healing. By integrating creativity into the fabric of society, we open doors to new perspectives, challenge existing paradigms, and celebrate the richness of the human experience.

Building Communities of Support: The foundation of a balanced society lies in its communities—spaces where individuals can find support, understanding, and a sense of belonging. Strengthening these communities through inclusive policies, empathetic leadership, and active participation can create environments where every individual has the opportunity to thrive.

As we look to the future, let us carry forward the lessons of this journey, weaving the threads of awareness, compassion, and connection into the societal fabric. The path forward is not without its challenges, but with each step taken in mindfulness and solidarity, we move closer to a society that embraces the full spectrum of human experience, offering not just paninis and circuses but a place at the table for every Pagliacci, where laughter and tears are met with equal reverence, and the pursuit of fulfillment transcends the distractions of the day.

Appendix

Resources for Mental Health Support

Global Resources:

1. World Health Organization (WHO): Provides comprehensive resources, including guidelines for seeking mental health care and a directory of national mental health programs and crisis helplines around the world.

2. Mental Health America (MHA): Offers a wide range of tools and information on mental health, including screening tools, educational materials, and advocacy resources.

3. International Association for Suicide Prevention (IASP): Features global resources for suicide prevention, including crisis centers and helplines.

United States:

1. National Alliance on Mental Illness (NAMI): Offers support, education, and advocacy for individuals with mental illness and their families. Helpline: 1-800-950-NAMI (6264).

2. Substance Abuse and Mental Health Services Administration (SAMHSA): Provides a national helpline for individuals facing mental health or substance use disorders. Helpline: 1-800-662-HELP (4357).

United Kingdom:

1. Mind: Provides advice and support to empower anyone experiencing a mental health problem. Helpline: 0300 123 3393.

2. Samaritans: Offers a safe place for anyone to talk any time they like, in their own way – about whatever's getting to them. Helpline: 116 123.

Australia:

1. Beyond Blue: Offers information and support to help everyone in Australia achieve their best possible mental health. Helpline: 1300 22 4636.

2. Lifeline: A national charity providing all Australians experiencing emotional distress with access to 24-hour crisis support and suicide prevention services. Helpline: 13 11 14.

Canada:

1. Crisis Services Canada: A national network of existing distress, crisis, and suicide prevention line services. Helpline: 1-833-456-4566.

Note: Many countries have their own mental health support systems and hotlines. It's important to seek out resources specific to your location.

Further Reading on the History of "Bread and Circuses"

1. "The Roman Circus: Arenas for Chariot Racing" by Katherine Welch: A detailed exploration of the significance of circus games in Roman culture and their impact on society.

2. "Entertainment & Society Around the World: Bread and Circuses" by Kenneth L. Campbell: Examines the concept of bread and circuses throughout history, analyzing its relevance in various societal contexts.

3. "Feeding Rome: The Politics of Feeding a Roman City" by David Mattingly and Gregory Aldrete: Provides insight into the political and social mechanisms behind the distribution of food in ancient Rome.

4. "The Fall of the Roman Empire: A New History of Rome and the Barbarians" by Peter Heather: Offers a comprehensive look at the factors contributing to the decline of the Roman Empire, including the role of public entertainment.

5. "Satire VI" by Juvenal: For a primary source perspective, Juvenal's Satire VI is where the phrase "bread and circuses" originates, offering a critique of Roman society's complacency.

These resources and readings offer a starting point for those seeking support for mental health issues or looking to deepen their understanding of the historical context and societal implications of "bread and circuses." Whether you're exploring the complexities of modern-day distractions or seeking ways to foster mental wellness, these tools and insights provide valuable guidance on the journey towards a more mindful and informed society.

Sun Tzu's The Art Of Personal Recovery
The Warrior's Journey to Self-Discovery and Recovery
Julian Del Bel

1. The Foundation of Self-Help Through Ancient Strategy
   - Understanding the Art of War
   - Adapting Ancient Principles for Modern Self-Improvement

2. Know Yourself: The Path to Internal Awareness
   - Discovering Your Inner Strengths and Weaknesses
   - Cultivating Self-Awareness and Honesty

3. Know Your Enemy: Confronting Your Challenges
   - Identifying Personal Obstacles and Adversaries
   - Strategies to Overcome Internal and External Conflicts

4. The Strategic Approach to Recovery
   - Planning Your Path to Improvement

- Flexibility and Adaptation in Personal Growth

5. Tactical Advancements in Self-Healing
   - Incremental Progress and Small Victories
   - The Importance of Tactical Withdrawal

6. The Terrain of Recovery: Navigating Your Environment
   - Understanding and Utilizing Your Surroundings
   - Creating a Supportive Environment for Growth

7. The Use of Spies: Gathering Information to Aid Recovery
   - Seeking Guidance and Wisdom from Others
   - Learning from Successes and Failures

8. The Attack by Fire: Igniting Passion and Determination
   - Cultivating Passion to Overcome Apathy
   - Using Determination as a Weapon Against Despair

9. The Unorthodox and Orthodox: Balancing Creativity and Discipline
   - The Role of Creativity in Solving Problems
   - The Importance of Discipline and Routine

10. Alliance and Diplomacy: Building Relationships to Support Recovery
    - Forming Strategic Alliances for Mutual Support
    - Navigating Relationships with Wisdom and Care

11. Leadership in Recovery: Guiding Yourself and Others
    - Being a Leader in Your Recovery Journey
    - Inspiring and Helping Others on Their Path

12. The Endless Path: Continuous Growth and Adaptation
    - Embracing Lifelong Learning and Growth
    - Adapting Strategies for Different Stages of Life

Conclusion: The Warrior's Journey to Self-Discovery and Recovery

- Integrating the Lessons of Sun Tzu into Everyday Life
- The Continuous Cycle of Learning, Growing, and Overcoming

Prelude:

In our relentless pursuit of personal growth and healing, we often find ourselves sifting through contemporary self-help methodologies, searching for that elusive key to unlock the door to our better selves. Yet, amidst this modern quest, there lies a treasure trove of wisdom in the ancient texts of the past, waiting to be rediscovered and applied to the challenges of our current existence. One such text is "The Art of War" by Sun Tzu, a masterpiece of military strategy and philosophy from 5th century BC China. While it may initially seem far removed from the sphere of personal recovery and self-improvement, a closer examination reveals that Sun Tzu's strategies for overcoming adversaries on the battlefield possess profound insights for those of us battling the internal foes of doubt, fear, and stagnation.

1. The Foundation of Self-Help Through Ancient Strategy

Understanding the Art of War

Sun Tzu's "The Art of War" is not merely a manual on the tactical elements of warfare; it is a profound treatise on the psychology of conflict, leadership, and the importance of strategic planning. The text delves into the nuances of assessing strengths and weaknesses, the significance of timing, and the value of knowledge – both of oneself and of the adversary. These concepts, though framed in the context of ancient military campaigns, resonate deeply with the internal struggles many face in their journey toward personal betterment.

At its essence, "The Art of War" teaches us that victory comes from within, advocating for a deep understanding of one's own capabilities and limitations, and a strategic approach to overcoming obstacles. This introspective wisdom serves as a powerful foundation for self-help, offering a unique lens through which we can examine our personal battles and the strategies we employ to confront them.

Adapting Ancient Principles for Modern Self-Improvement

This book is an exploration of how Sun Tzu's ancient wisdom can be repurposed for the modern individual's quest for recovery and growth. Each chapter dissects a core principle of "The Art of War" and reinterprets it for the internal and external challenges we face in the contemporary world. From the process of self-discovery and the recognition of our personal demons, to the strategies we can employ to navigate the complex emotional landscapes of our lives, Sun Tzu's teachings provide a timeless framework for confronting and overcoming our difficulties.

The journey toward self-improvement is akin to navigating a battlefield, where each challenge or setback represents an adversary to be strategically engaged with. Sun Tzu's emphasis on preparation, knowledge, and adaptability is particularly relevant here; by applying these principles, we learn to approach our personal development with the strategic mindset of a seasoned general, turning our weaknesses into strengths and our failures into stepping stones for success.

Sun Tzu's concept of victory through strategic superiority rather than brute force invites us to consider how we can achieve our goals through wisdom, patience, and cunning, rather than overwhelming effort or sheer willpower alone. This nuanced approach to personal recovery encourages us to find balance, seek alignment with our true selves, and embrace the power of strategic thinking in our everyday lives.

As we investigate the ancient wisdom of Sun Tzu, let us embark on a transformative journey of self-discovery, armed with the strategies of the past to conquer the challenges of the present. By bridging the gap between the timeless tactics of "The Art of War" and the modern quest for personal growth, this book aims to guide readers through their own personal battles, offering a path to victory that is as much about inner harmony as it is about outward success. Through this exploration, we may find that the greatest wars are not fought on the battlefields of old, but within the vast, untamed territories of the human soul.

2. Know Yourself: The Path to Internal Awareness

The journey to self-improvement and personal recovery is underpinned by a fundamental principle that echoes through the ages, finding profound expression in Sun Tzu's "The Art of War": "Know yourself and know your enemy, and you will never be in peril." This chapter delves deep into the first half of this timeless strategy—knowing oneself. In the context of personal development, the 'enemy' often manifests as our internal struggles, and understanding these begins with a deep, introspective dive into our own psyche. This exploration is twofold: discovering our inner strengths and weaknesses, and cultivating self-awareness and honesty.

Discovering Your Inner Strengths and Weaknesses

The path to self-discovery is not a journey outward but inward. It is a voyage into the deepest recesses of our being to unearth the truths about who we are. This process requires us to confront both our strengths and weaknesses, acknowledging them not as definitive judgments of our character but as aspects of our humanity that can be harnessed or improved.

Strengths are the bedrock upon which we can build a resilient and victorious self. They are the unique talents, attributes, and qualities that empower us to face life's challenges with confidence and grace. Recognizing these strengths is not an exercise in vanity but a crucial step in understanding how we can contribute positively to our own lives and the lives of others.

Weaknesses, on the other hand, are often perceived negatively, shadows of our character that we wish to hide or eliminate. However, acknowledging our weaknesses is just as important as recognizing our strengths. Weaknesses are not immutable flaws but areas for potential growth and development. They guide us in understanding where we may need to focus our efforts in self-improvement, whether it be developing new skills, seeking knowledge, or working to change certain behaviors.

Cultivating Self-Awareness and Honesty

The process of discovering our inner strengths and weaknesses necessitates a high degree of self-awareness. This involves an ongoing, honest dialogue with oneself, a willingness to ask difficult questions, and the courage to face uncomfortable truths. Cultivating self-awareness means paying attention to our thoughts, emotions, and behaviors. It requires mindfulness and reflection, qualities that allow us to observe our actions and their impact without immediate judgment or criticism.

Honesty is the linchpin of self-awareness. It is the quality that allows us to see ourselves clearly, without the distortion of ego or the shadows of self-deception. Being honest with ourselves is not an easy task; it demands vulnerability and a readiness to confront aspects of our character we may not be proud of. However, it is only through this honesty that we can truly know ourselves and begin the process of transformation.

Practical Steps for Cultivating Self-Awareness and Honesty

1. Journaling: Regularly writing down your thoughts and feelings can provide valuable insights into your inner world. It serves as a mirror, reflecting your true self back to you.

2. Meditation and Mindfulness: Practices that encourage presence and awareness can help you become more attuned to your internal state, aiding in the recognition of your thoughts and emotions as they arise.

3. Feedback from Trusted Individuals: Sometimes, an outside perspective can reveal aspects of ourselves that we are blind to. Engaging with close friends, family, or mentors who can offer constructive and honest feedback is invaluable.

4. Exploration of Your Values: Understanding what you truly value can shed light on your motivations and guide you towards greater alignment between your actions and your deepest beliefs.

As we embark on this journey of self-discovery, let us remember that knowing oneself is not a destination but a continuous process. It is a path paved with the stones of introspection, honesty, and the unwavering commitment to personal growth. Through this process, we not only prepare ourselves to face our external 'enemies' but also cultivate the internal fortitude necessary to overcome the obstacles that lie within.

3. Know Your Enemy: Confronting Your Challenges

The quest for personal betterment is a journey fraught with adversaries, both seen and unseen, that obstruct our path toward self-realization and fulfillment. Drawing from Sun Tzu's ancient wisdom, to "know your enemy" becomes a metaphorical call to arms in our personal battles. It compels us to engage deeply with the challenges that deter us, understanding that the landscape of our struggles is often a complex terrain of internal fears and external pressures. This chapter seeks to explore the nuanced facets of identifying and overcoming these challenges, illuminating strategies that empower us to navigate through the storms of our lives.

Identifying Personal Obstacles and Adversaries

The art of knowing one's enemy begins with identification. Our adversaries manifest in various forms, ranging from the deeply ingrained beliefs that limit our potential, to the external conditions that challenge our resolve. The task of identification is thus twofold, demanding a keen introspection to unearth the internal foes and a critical observation to recognize the external forces at play.

Internal Obstacles: The battleground of the mind is often where the fiercest wars are waged. Our inner adversaries are shadowy figures, forged from the fabric of our fears, doubts, and insecurities. They whisper tales of inadequacy, stoke the flames of procrastination, and chain us with the weight of past failures. These are the voices that seek to undermine our confidence, the patterns that drive us into cycles of self-sabotage, and the beliefs that narrow our vision of what is truly possible. To confront them, we must shine a light on these shadows, acknowledging their presence not as invincible foes but as facets of our being that can be understood, challenged, and transformed.

External Adversaries: Beyond the confines of our psyche lie the external forces that shape our journey. These include not only the people and relationships that may drain our energy but also the societal structures and cultural expectations that dictate how we should live, work, and even love. The obstacles here are multifaceted, encompassing everything from financial hardships and career challenges to broader societal injustices and global crises. Recognizing these forces requires a discerning eye, one that can see beyond the immediate to understand the broader context of our struggles, empowering us to navigate these waters with strategic grace.

Strategies to Overcome Internal and External Conflicts

With our adversaries laid bare, the next step is to marshal our resources and devise strategies to surmount these obstacles. This endeavor requires not just strength but wisdom, creativity, and a deep commitment to self-evolution.

Strategies for Internal Obstacles:

1. Cultivate Self-Compassion: Begin by forging an alliance with yourself through the power of self-compassion. Treat yourself with the same kindness and understanding you would offer a dear friend. This nurturing approach can transform the inner battlefield into a ground of healing and growth.

2. Engage in Mindful Reframing: Challenge the narratives spun by your internal adversaries. Mindful reframing allows you to alter your perception, recognizing that the power to redefine your story lies within you. By changing your internal dialogue, you change the course of your battle.

3. Embrace Mental and Emotional Flexibility: The ability to adapt your thoughts and emotions in response to changing circumstances is akin to the strategic flexibility lauded by Sun Tzu. Cultivate this agility to turn perceived weaknesses into strengths and to find opportunities amidst adversity.

4. Pursue Inner Harmony: Seek practices that ground you in a state of calm and clarity, whether through meditation, nature walks, or artistic expression. Inner peace is your sanctuary, offering respite and renewal amidst the chaos.

Strategies for External Conflicts:

1. Adopt Strategic Planning: Foresee potential challenges and prepare accordingly. Strategic planning involves not just the anticipation of obstacles but also the preparation for various outcomes, allowing you to navigate with confidence.

2. Forge Alliances: Build a coalition of support by connecting with individuals who uplift and inspire you. These alliances are your reinforcements, offering strength, advice, and solace in times of need.

3. Exercise Adaptability: Be willing to alter your tactics as the terrain of your external world shifts. Adaptability is a hallmark of strategic mastery, enabling you to maneuver through life's uncertainties with dexterity.

4. Concentrate on Controllable Elements: While you may not have dominion over every aspect of your external environment, you retain control over your actions and reactions. Focusing on what you can influence cultivates a sense of agency and empowerment.

By embarking on this comprehensive approach to knowing and confronting our enemies, we embrace a holistic strategy for personal growth and recovery. This path is not about waging war against ourselves or the world but about understanding and navigating the complexities of our existence with wisdom, courage, and strategic insight. In doing so, we not only overcome the challenges before us but also transform them into stepping stones on our journey to becoming our most authentic and empowered selves.

4. The Strategic Approach to Recovery

The journey of personal recovery and growth is an expedition that demands not only courage and resilience but also strategic wisdom. This wisdom, as Sun Tzu might suggest, lies not in seeking battle but in preparing the ground for victory long before the fight begins. A strategic approach to recovery involves meticulous planning, coupled with the agility to adapt to the ever-changing landscapes of our lives. This chapter delves into the essence of crafting a strategic path toward self-improvement, emphasizing the dual pillars of planning and flexibility as the bedrock of personal growth.

Planning Your Path to Improvement

Strategic planning in the context of personal recovery and growth is an introspective process that goes beyond mere goal setting. It involves a comprehensive understanding of one's current position, a clear vision of the desired outcome, and a detailed mapping of the journey from here to there. This process is akin to a general surveying the battlefield, assessing the terrain, the strengths and weaknesses of his forces, and those of the enemy, before devising a plan of attack.

1. Assessment: The first step in planning your path to improvement is a thorough self-assessment. This involves taking stock of your current state—identifying your strengths, acknowledging your weaknesses, understanding your needs, and recognizing the obstacles that stand in your way. It's about gaining a clear and honest understanding of where you are on your journey.

2. Vision: With a solid grasp of your starting point, the next step is to articulate a clear vision of where you want to go. This vision should be specific, measurable, achievable, relevant, and time-bound (SMART). It should resonate with your values and aspirations, serving as a guiding star on your path to recovery.

3. Strategic Goals: From this vision, derive strategic goals that act as milestones on your journey. These goals should be structured in a way that they lead you step by step towards your ultimate destination. Each goal should address specific areas of improvement, recovery, or growth, and should be accompanied by actionable steps that move you closer to your vision.

4. Resource Allocation: Planning also involves considering the resources at your disposal—time, energy, support networks, and material resources—and how best to allocate them to achieve your goals. This might include setting aside time for self-care, seeking out support groups, or investing in tools and education that facilitate your growth.

5. Contingency Plans: A strategic plan is incomplete without consideration of potential setbacks and obstacles. Developing contingency plans involves thinking through what might go wrong and how to address it without derailing your progress. It's about being prepared for the unexpected and having a plan B (and even a plan C) ready.

Flexibility and Adaptation in Personal Growth

While planning provides the roadmap for our journey, flexibility and adaptation are the skills that allow us to navigate it successfully. The path to recovery is rarely linear; it is filled with unforeseen challenges and opportunities that require us to be nimble and responsive.

1. Embracing Change: Flexibility in personal growth means being open to change and willing to adjust your plans as you learn and evolve. It's about recognizing that what works today

may not work tomorrow, and being prepared to pivot in response to new information or circumstances.

2. Learning from Setbacks: Adaptation involves viewing setbacks not as failures but as learning opportunities. Each challenge we encounter is a chance to gather intelligence about ourselves and our journey, allowing us to refine our strategies and become more resilient.

3. Innovative Problem-Solving: Flexibility and adaptation call for creativity in overcoming obstacles. This might involve thinking outside the box to find solutions, leveraging new tools or approaches, or seeking out alternative paths to your goals.

4. Mindful Persistence: Being flexible does not mean being aimless. It's about maintaining a clear focus on your vision while being adaptable in your methods. This mindful persistence ensures that even as you adjust your plans, you remain anchored to your ultimate objectives.

By intertwining strategic planning with the ability to flex and adapt, we equip ourselves for the journey of personal recovery and growth. This approach allows us to navigate the complexities and uncertainties of our paths with confidence, ensuring that each step we take is both considered and agile. As we traverse this journey, let us remember that the art of strategy lies not in the avoidance of challenges but in the mastery of them, transforming each obstacle into a stepping stone towards our desired future.

5. Tactical Advancements in Self-Healing

In the intricate dance of personal recovery and self-improvement, our progress often mirrors the subtle, strategic maneuvers of a carefully planned military campaign. Drawing deeply from the ancient wisdom of Sun Tzu's "The Art of War," this chapter unfolds the art of tactical advancements in the realm of self-healing. It reveals the profound power of embracing incremental progress and small victories, along with the strategic necessity of tactical withdrawal, as pivotal elements in the journey towards wellness and personal growth.

Incremental Progress and Small Victories

Crafting a Path of Measured Steps

The journey towards healing and self-improvement is rarely marked by swift, dramatic leaps. Instead, it is the accumulation of small, deliberate steps that pave the way to meaningful change. This concept of incremental progress is akin to laying bricks to construct a path; each brick may seem insignificant on its own, but together, they create a solid road leading to our desired destination.

Celebrating Small Victories as Milestones

Within this journey, the small victories we achieve serve as beacons of progress, lighting our way and uplifting our spirits. These moments—whether overcoming a personal fear, making a difficult decision that aligns with our values, or simply maintaining a new healthy habit—are milestones that deserve recognition and celebration. They remind us of our capacity for change and resilience, reinforcing our commitment to the path we have chosen.

The Cumulative Effect of Incremental Change

The power of incremental progress lies in its ability to produce significant, lasting transformation over time. Like the slow sculpting of landscapes by the steady drip of water, each small action we take in service of our recovery and growth contributes to the grand tapestry of our lives. This approach not only makes the process of personal development more manageable but also embeds the changes deeply within us, ensuring they are sustainable and integrated into our very being.

The Importance of Tactical Withdrawal

Embracing the Strategic Pause

In the relentless pursuit of growth, the wisdom of tactical withdrawal serves as a reminder of the importance of rest, reflection, and recalibration. This strategic pause is not a sign of weakness or failure but a vital component of a sustainable journey towards self-improvement. It allows us to conserve energy, evaluate our progress, and rejuvenate our spirits, ensuring that we can continue our pursuit with renewed vigor and clarity.

The Role of Reflection in Reassessment

A tactical withdrawal provides a valuable opportunity for deep reflection on our journey thus far. It invites us to assess the strategies we have employed, the obstacles we have encountered, and the victories we have secured. This period of introspection enables us to identify what has been effective, what needs adjustment, and how we might better align our actions with our goals moving forward.

Adapting Strategies for Continued Growth

The insights gained during periods of tactical withdrawal are instrumental in adapting our approach to recovery and growth. They allow us to pivot our strategies, experiment with new methods, and embrace flexibility in our path. This adaptability is crucial in navigating the unpredictable and often challenging landscape of personal development, ensuring that we remain resilient and responsive to the changing tides of our journey.

The nuanced approach to self-healing, grounded in the principles of incremental progress and tactical withdrawal, offers a powerful framework for navigating the complex process of personal recovery. It acknowledges that the path to wellness is both a battlefield and a sanctuary, requiring the courage to advance and the wisdom to retreat. By embodying the tactical finesse of a seasoned warrior, we equip ourselves with the tools necessary to forge ahead in our journey towards healing, growth, and the ultimate realization of our fullest potential.

6. The Terrain of Recovery: Navigating Your Environment

In the landscape of personal recovery and growth, our environment plays a pivotal role, much like the terrain on a battlefield influences the strategies of ancient warfare as outlined by Sun Tzu in "The Art of War." This chapter delves into the importance of understanding and utilizing our surroundings in the context of personal development, alongside strategies for creating a supportive environment that nurtures growth and healing. Drawing on Sun Tzu's wisdom, we explore how the metaphorical terrain of our lives—comprising physical, social, and psychological spaces—can significantly impact our journey towards recovery.

Understanding and Utilizing Your Surroundings

Our environment encompasses more than just the physical space around us; it includes the people we interact with, the information we consume, and the general atmosphere that influences our daily lives. Just as a general must understand the terrain to plan a successful campaign, we too must recognize the impact of our surroundings on our recovery journey.

Physical Environment: The spaces where we spend our time can profoundly affect our mood, energy levels, and overall mental health. Cluttered, chaotic environments may contribute to stress and anxiety, while calm, organized spaces can promote a sense of peace and focus. Assessing and adjusting our physical surroundings to support our well-being is a crucial step in creating a conducive environment for recovery.

Social Environment: The people we surround ourselves with can act as allies or adversaries on our path to growth. Supportive relationships provide encouragement, understanding, and companionship, offering a buffer against the challenges we face. Conversely, toxic relationships can drain our energy and impede our progress. Cultivating a network of supportive individuals who respect our journey and contribute positively to our recovery is essential.

Psychological Environment: The information we consume and the thoughts we entertain shape our internal landscape. Exposure to negative media, destructive self-talk, and limiting beliefs can create a hostile environment for growth. Conversely, consuming positive, uplifting content and practicing affirmations can reinforce our recovery efforts. Being mindful of the psychological atmosphere we create for ourselves is key to fostering a mindset conducive to healing.

Creating a Supportive Environment for Growth

Once we understand the significant role our environment plays in our recovery, the next step is to actively create a setting that supports our growth. This process involves both modifying our current surroundings and cultivating habits that reinforce a positive and nurturing atmosphere.

Designing a Healing Space: Begin by creating physical spaces that reflect tranquility, inspiration, and comfort. This might involve decluttering living areas, incorporating elements of nature, or setting up a dedicated space for meditation or reflection. Personalizing your environment to suit your healing needs can transform it into a sanctuary that supports your recovery journey.

Cultivating Positive Relationships: Actively seek out and nurture relationships with individuals who uplift and support you. This could mean deepening connections with empathetic friends and family, joining support groups, or seeking out mentors who have navigated similar paths. Surrounding yourself with a community of support acts as a powerful force multiplier in your recovery efforts.

Nurturing a Positive Mindset: Your psychological environment is perhaps the most critical to master. Engage in practices that cultivate a positive mindset, such as mindfulness meditation, journaling, and gratitude exercises. Limit exposure to negative media and conversations, and intentionally fill your mental space with uplifting and motivational content.

Adapting to Environmental Changes: Just as Sun Tzu advises flexibility in response to changing battlefield conditions, be prepared to adapt your environmental strategies as your recovery journey evolves. Regularly assess the effectiveness of your surroundings in supporting your growth and make adjustments as necessary. This dynamic approach ensures that your environment continues to serve your healing process, no matter the circumstances.

Navigating the terrain of recovery requires a strategic approach to understanding and shaping our environment in ways that support our journey. By carefully curating our physical, social, and psychological spaces, we can create a fertile ground for personal growth, resilience, and transformation. This chapter aims to guide readers through the process of assessing and optimizing their surroundings, drawing on the timeless wisdom of Sun Tzu to navigate the complex terrain of recovery with strategic insight and purpose.

7. The Use of Spies: Gathering Information to Aid Recovery

In "The Art of War," Sun Tzu emphasizes the critical role of espionage in gaining the upper hand in conflict situations. Translating this concept into the context of personal recovery and growth, "The Use of Spies" can be metaphorically understood as the process of gathering information and insights that can aid in our journey towards self-improvement. This chapter explores the importance of seeking guidance and wisdom from others, as well as learning from both our successes and failures, to inform and enhance our recovery strategies.

Seeking Guidance and Wisdom from Others

In the pursuit of personal recovery, external perspectives and expertise can offer invaluable insights that might not be apparent from our vantage point. Just as spies provide crucial information about the enemy and the terrain, trusted individuals in our lives can offer perspectives and advice that illuminate our path and help us navigate our challenges more effectively.

Mentors and Guides: Identifying mentors or guides who have navigated similar paths or possess the wisdom we seek is crucial. These individuals can act as beacons, offering guidance, support, and encouragement. Their experiences can serve as a roadmap, highlighting potential pitfalls and effective strategies that might accelerate our journey toward wellness.

Professional Help: Sometimes, the guidance we need comes from professionals who specialize in helping individuals overcome the particular challenges we face. Therapists, counselors, and coaches can offer tailored strategies and tools to manage our struggles, providing a structured environment for our recovery.

Community and Support Groups: Engaging with communities or support groups consisting of individuals facing similar challenges can also be profoundly beneficial. These spaces offer not only empathy and understanding but also a wealth of shared experiences from which to draw lessons and encouragement.

Learning from Successes and Failures

The journey of recovery is punctuated by both successes and setbacks. Each of these instances provides valuable data points, much like the reports spies deliver to their commanders. Analyzing and understanding these outcomes can significantly inform and refine our recovery strategies.

Reflecting on Successes: Every success, no matter how small, offers insights into what works. It's essential to take the time to analyze these victories, understanding the factors that contributed to the success. This reflection can help reinforce effective strategies and boost confidence in our ability to overcome obstacles.

Analyzing Failures: Similarly, setbacks and failures are not mere stumbling blocks but opportunities for learning and growth. By adopting a non-judgmental and analytical approach to understanding what didn't work and why we can extract lessons that refine our approach to recovery. This process of learning from failure is crucial in developing resilience and adaptability.

Adaptive Learning: The ultimate goal is to become adept at adaptive learning — the ability to quickly assimilate the lessons from both successes and failures and apply them to future situations. This dynamic process of learning and adapting ensures that our recovery strategies are continually refined and optimized for the challenges we face.

The use of "spies" in our recovery journey is a metaphor for the proactive gathering of information, insights, and perspectives that can illuminate our path forward. By seeking guidance and wisdom from others and learning from our experiences, we equip ourselves with the knowledge and understanding necessary to navigate the complexities of personal growth. This chapter underscores the importance of being open to external input and reflective in our approach, ensuring that every step taken is informed and intentional.

8. The Attack by Fire: Igniting Passion and Determination

In the transformative journey of self-improvement and recovery, invoking the "attack by fire" strategy, inspired by Sun Tzu's "The Art of War," becomes a powerful metaphor for igniting the inner forces of passion and determination. This chapter explores the intricate process of cultivating these dynamic qualities to combat the paralyzing grip of apathy and despair. It delves into how we can stoke the embers of our deepest desires and leverage unwavering resolve as a weapon against the darkness that threatens to undermine our progress. Through this exploration, we aim to fan the flames of our inner fire, propelling us forward on the path to healing, growth, and fulfillment.

Cultivating Passion to Overcome Apathy

Apathy acts as a silent adversary in our quest for self-betterment, numbing our senses and stifling our motivation with its cold embrace. Overcoming this state demands more than mere intention; it requires the kindling of passion, that fervent energy driving us toward our goals with vitality and zeal.

Discovering Your Fire Within: The quest for passion begins with a journey inward, to the core of our being, where our deepest desires and values lie dormant, waiting to be awakened. This exploration involves peeling back the layers of our identity and experiences to reveal the essence of what truly moves us. Engaging in self-reflective practices such as journaling, meditation, or creative expression can illuminate these hidden passions, offering a glimpse into the forces that can drive our recovery and growth.

Nurturing Your Passions Through Engagement: Identifying your passions is only the first step; nurturing them requires active engagement and cultivation. This involves seeking out and creating opportunities to immerse yourself in the activities, ideas, and pursuits that resonate with your core interests. Whether it's through hobbies, learning new skills, or engaging in meaningful work, the process of engagement keeps the flame of passion alive, providing a bulwark against the encroaching chill of apathy.

Using Determination as a Weapon Against Despair

While passion provides the spark for action, it is determination that sustains the journey, especially when faced with adversity. Determination acts as the steady hand guiding us through storms, a testament to our resilience and commitment to persevere.

Forging Determination Through Goal Setting and Visualization: The bedrock of determination is often found in the clarity of our goals and the vision we hold for our future.

Setting clear, attainable objectives not only outlines the path forward but also serves as a source of motivation, keeping us anchored to our purpose. Visualization techniques can further enhance this process, allowing us to embody the success and fulfillment we aspire to achieve, thus reinforcing our resolve to press onward.

Cultivating a Mindset of Resilience: True determination is rooted in a resilient mindset, one that embraces challenges as avenues for growth and learning. Developing such a mindset involves practicing gratitude, engaging in positive self-talk, and learning to view failures not as setbacks but as integral steps in the learning process. This perspective shift can transform despair into determination, fueling our journey with a renewed sense of purpose and possibility.

Leveraging Community and Support Systems: No battle is fought alone, and the journey towards self-improvement is no exception. Building a network of support—be it through friends, family, mentors, or support groups—can significantly bolster our determination. These relationships provide encouragement, offer different perspectives, and hold us accountable, all of which are essential in maintaining our momentum and focus.

The strategy of "the attack by fire" is thus a comprehensive approach to igniting and sustaining the inner forces of passion and determination. It recognizes that the journey of self-improvement is fraught with challenges but asserts that within us lies the power to overcome them. By actively cultivating passion and harnessing determination, we arm ourselves with the tools necessary to traverse the path of recovery and growth. This chapter serves as a guide to lighting that fire within, ensuring that even in the face of apathy and despair, we can find the strength to continue moving forward, burning brighter and more fiercely than ever before.

9. The Unorthodox and Orthodox: Balancing Creativity and Discipline

In the multifaceted journey of personal growth and recovery, the strategic interplay between creativity (the unorthodox) and discipline (the orthodox), as inspired by the ancient wisdom of Sun Tzu in "The Art of War," emerges as a pivotal theme. This delicate balance between the fluidity of creative thought and the rigidity of disciplined action serves as a foundational strategy for navigating the complexities of self-improvement. By embracing both the unorthodox and orthodox methods, we are afforded a comprehensive toolkit that enhances our ability to problem-solve, adapt, and evolve on our path to personal fulfillment and resilience. This chapter delves into the nuanced roles that creativity and discipline play in the process of personal development, offering insights into how their harmonious integration can lead to a more enriched and effective journey toward self-betterment.

The Role of Creativity in Solving Problems

Creativity, the essence of the unorthodox approach, empowers us to transcend conventional thinking and explore the realms of what could be. It is the creative spark that illuminates new paths and uncovers innovative solutions to the challenges that impede our progress.

Embracing the Power of Lateral Thinking: Lateral thinking, a concept closely tied to creativity, involves looking at problems from new and often unexpected angles. It encourages us to break free from traditional patterns of thought and to explore a broader range of solutions. By fostering lateral thinking, we open ourselves up to a diverse array of strategies and approaches that can be tailored to meet the unique demands of our personal growth journey.

The Transformative Potential of Creative Expression: Creative expression, whether through art, writing, music, or any other form, serves as a conduit for exploring our inner landscape and bringing to light the emotions, thoughts, and desires that drive us. This process of expression not only offers therapeutic benefits but also enhances our problem-solving skills by providing a tangible outlet for abstract ideas and feelings, thereby contributing to our overall well-being and self-awareness.

The Importance of Discipline and Routine

In contrast to the boundless nature of creativity, discipline introduces a structured approach to personal development, emphasizing the importance of routine, consistency, and self-control.

Cultivating a Habit of Persistence: Discipline teaches us the value of persistence in the face of obstacles. It is through the disciplined application of effort over time that we are able to manifest our goals and aspirations. By developing a habit of persistence, we build the resilience necessary to navigate setbacks and continue forward, even when progress seems slow or uncertain.

The Role of Routine in Sustaining Momentum: Establishing a routine is a fundamental aspect of discipline that helps sustain momentum in our journey. A well-structured routine not only provides a sense of stability and predictability but also ensures that we are consistently dedicating time and energy toward our objectives. Through routine, we create a disciplined framework that supports sustained effort and progress.

Balancing Creativity and Discipline: A Dynamic Equilibrium

The dynamic equilibrium between creativity and discipline is where the magic of personal growth and recovery happens. This balance allows us to harness the full spectrum of our capabilities, leveraging the spontaneity of creative thought and the stability of disciplined action to navigate our journey with wisdom and adaptability.

Implementing Creative Solutions Within a Disciplined Framework: One effective strategy for balancing creativity and discipline involves implementing creative solutions within a disciplined framework. This approach allows for the exploration of innovative ideas while ensuring that these ideas are pursued with systematic effort and consistency.

Adapting to Change with Flexibility and Structure: Balancing creativity and discipline also means being adaptable to change while maintaining a structured approach to our goals. Flexibility enables us to respond to the unexpected with grace, while discipline ensures that we remain focused and committed to our path, regardless of the obstacles we encounter.

By integrating the unorthodox and orthodox approaches to personal development, we equip ourselves with a comprehensive set of tools for tackling the challenges of self-improvement. Creativity and discipline, though seemingly at odds, are in fact complementary forces that, when balanced, provide the key to unlocking our full potential and achieving lasting transformation on our journey to recovery and beyond.

10. Alliance and Diplomacy: Building Relationships to Support Recovery

In the labyrinthine journey of personal development and recovery, the strategic formation and nurturing of relationships stand as pivotal elements, drawing a parallel to the ancient strategies of alliance and diplomacy championed by Sun Tzu. This expansive exploration delves into the nuanced art of cultivating strategic alliances for mutual support and navigating the intricate dynamics of these relationships with profound wisdom and meticulous care. It underscores how, akin to the coalitions between nations, our interpersonal connections can emerge as formidable bastions of support, propelling us towards our goals with added strength and resilience. Through the prism of diplomacy, we learn to manage these ties with grace, ensuring they enrich our journey towards self-improvement.

Forming Strategic Alliances for Mutual Support

The tapestry of human connection is rich and diverse, offering a plethora of opportunities for forming alliances that bolster our spirits and fortify our resolve. These strategic alliances are not mere happenstance but are fostered through deliberate intention and shared purpose, echoing the alliances of old where common goals united disparate entities.

Expanding the Circle of Allies: Venturing beyond the confines of familiar social territories to identify allies demands openness and a keen sense of discernment. Potential allies may be discovered in unexpected places, from workshops and seminars aligned with our interests, to online communities and support networks. The act of reaching out, initiating conversations, and participating in shared experiences lays the groundwork for meaningful connections.

The Alchemy of Relationship Building: The transformation of acquaintances into allies is an alchemy that requires patience, shared experiences, and the mutual exchange of value and support. It calls for an investment of time and energy, nurturing these connections with the nutrients of empathy, understanding, and mutual respect. As these bonds deepen, they evolve into a robust network of support, characterized by trust and a shared commitment to growth.

The Symbiosis of Support: Within the ecosystem of strategic alliances, support flows in a symbiotic cycle, nourishing all members. This reciprocity, a give-and-take dynamic, ensures that the relationship is balanced and sustainable. Being an active participant, offering support, and being receptive to receiving help in return, strengthens the alliance and fosters a sense of community and belonging.

Navigating Relationships with Wisdom and Care

The domain of diplomacy in personal relationships entails navigating the complexities of human interactions with a blend of tact, insight, and compassion. It demands a balance between expressing our authentic selves and being receptive to the needs and perspectives of others.

The Art of Communication: Mastering the art of communication is critical in maintaining healthy, supportive relationships. This involves not just the articulation of thoughts and feelings but also the cultivation of active listening skills. Diplomatic communication seeks to bridge gaps, clarify misunderstandings, and build a foundation of mutual respect and understanding.

Boundaries as Pillars of Respect: The delineation and respect of personal boundaries are paramount in any healthy relationship. Diplomacy involves negotiating these boundaries with care, ensuring that they are respected and upheld. This negotiation requires clear communication, mutual understanding, and respect for individual needs and limitations.

Conflict Resolution with Grace: Conflicts, when navigated with diplomacy and tact, can become catalysts for deeper understanding and growth. Approaching disagreements with a willingness to understand the other's perspective, seeking common ground, and striving for resolutions that respect both parties' needs, are hallmarks of diplomatic conflict resolution.

Harmonizing Individual and Collective Needs: Maintaining a delicate balance between nurturing personal growth and contributing to the growth of the relationship is a dynamic challenge. It involves a continuous negotiation of space, time, and energy, ensuring that neither the individual nor the relationship is neglected. This balancing act requires ongoing communication, flexibility, and a deep commitment to mutual support.

The intricate dance of alliance and diplomacy in personal relationships is a testament to the power of human connection in supporting our journeys of recovery and self-improvement. By strategically forming and carefully navigating these relationships, we not only enrich our own lives but also contribute to the collective well-being of our communities. This chapter serves as a comprehensive guide to harnessing the transformative power of relationships, advocating for a balanced approach that combines the heart's warmth with the mind's clarity, propelling us towards our goals with the combined strength of our alliances.

12. The Endless Path: Continuous Growth and Adaptation

The journey of self-improvement and personal recovery is an enduring voyage that spans the entirety of our lives, a testament to the human spirit's resilience and its perpetual quest for growth. Drawing from the strategic depth of Sun Tzu's "The Art of War," this chapter ventures beyond the confines of conventional growth narratives to explore the boundless terrain of lifelong learning and the imperative of adapting our strategies through the diverse stages of life. It underscores the notion that personal development is not a destination but a continuous journey of evolution, requiring an unwavering commitment to adaptability, learning, and self-reflection.

Embracing Lifelong Learning and Growth

In the grand tapestry of human existence, the threads of lifelong learning weave a pattern of endless curiosity and exploration. This pursuit is not merely academic but encompasses the full spectrum of personal and experiential growth, enriching our lives with wisdom, skill, and understanding.

Fostering Intellectual Curiosity: A linchpin of lifelong learning is the cultivation of an insatiable intellectual curiosity. This involves actively seeking out new knowledge, challenging our existing beliefs, and remaining open to diverse perspectives. It's about embracing the joy of discovery and the excitement of uncovering the unknown, whether through reading, exploration, or engaging in stimulating conversations.

Integrating Learning into Daily Life: Lifelong learning is most effective when integrated into the fabric of our daily lives. This can mean setting aside time for self-study, incorporating educational podcasts or audiobooks into our routines, or engaging in hobbies that stretch our abilities and push us out of our comfort zones. The goal is to make learning a constant, vibrant thread in the narrative of our lives.

Embracing Change as a Catalyst for Growth: The only constant in life is change, and embracing this change is crucial for lifelong learning. Each shift in our personal or professional lives presents an opportunity to learn something new about ourselves and the world around us. By viewing change as a catalyst for growth, we transform potential obstacles into stepping stones on our path to self-discovery and improvement.

Adapting Strategies for Different Stages of Life

Life's journey is marked by a series of stages, each with its own set of challenges, opportunities, and lessons. Adapting our strategies for growth to these evolving stages ensures that our pursuit of personal development remains relevant, vibrant, and aligned with our changing needs and circumstances.

Navigating the Waters of Youth and Early Adulthood: This stage is characterized by exploration, identity formation, and the laying of foundations for future paths. Strategies here focus on expanding horizons, experimenting with different roles and identities, and developing a robust sense of self-awareness. It's a time for daring to dream big, while also cultivating the resilience to bounce back from the inevitable trials and errors of youth.

Midlife: A Time for Reevaluation and Reinvention: As we transition into midlife, we often find ourselves questioning earlier choices and contemplating new directions. This stage calls for strategies centered on introspection, reevaluation, and possibly, reinvention. It's an opportunity to realign our lives with our core values and passions, making deliberate changes to enhance our sense of fulfillment and purpose.

Embracing the Wisdom of Later Years: In the later years of life, our focus often shifts toward legacy, meaning, and imparting wisdom. The strategies during this stage involve reflecting on life's lessons, mentoring the next generation, and engaging in activities that leave a positive imprint on the world. It's a time for celebrating the journey, acknowledging the growth, and savoring the depth of experience that comes with a life well-lived.

Throughout this endless path of growth and adaptation, we are called to approach each stage with an open heart and a strategic mind, ready to embrace the lessons and opportunities that come our way. This chapter serves as a beacon, guiding us through the evolving landscape of our lives, reminding us that the pursuit of personal development is an infinite journey, rich with the potential for continuous learning, transformation, and renewal.

Conclusion: The Warrior's Journey to Self-Discovery and Recovery

Embarking on the journey of self-discovery and recovery is akin to the path of an ancient warrior, guided by the strategic wisdom of Sun Tzu. This profound expedition demands not just the courage to face external adversities but also the resolve to confront the inner landscapes of our being. It's a voyage that intertwines the art of warfare with the art of living, challenging us to integrate the timeless lessons of "The Art of War" into the fabric of our daily existence. This closing chapter seeks to distill the essence of our exploration, emphasizing the cyclical nature of learning, growing, and overcoming, as we navigate the intricate tapestry of human experience.

Integrating the Lessons of Sun Tzu into Everyday Life

The application of Sun Tzu's teachings to our personal lives transforms the way we perceive and engage with the world. It instills in us a strategic mindset, enabling us to approach life's challenges with wisdom, foresight, and a deep understanding of the human condition.

Living with Strategic Intent: Sun Tzu's emphasis on strategy extends beyond the battlefield to the realm of personal development. To live strategically is to navigate life with intent and purpose, making conscious choices that align with our deepest values and aspirations. It involves recognizing the interconnectedness of our actions and their ripple effects on our journey towards self-improvement.

The Fluidity of Adaptation: The teachings of Sun Tzu advocate for a fluid approach to life, one that is responsive to the ever-changing dynamics of our environment. This adaptability is crucial in an unpredictable world, where the only certainty is change itself. Embracing this fluidity allows us to remain resilient in the face of adversity, transforming potential setbacks into opportunities for growth.

Cultivating Deep Self-Awareness: The cornerstone of Sun Tzu's philosophy lies in the imperative to "know thyself." This journey towards self-awareness is both introspective and outward-facing, urging us to explore the depths of our psyche while remaining attuned to the world around us. It's a continuous process of reflection, learning, and self-reconciliation that empowers us to lead lives of authenticity and purpose.

The Continuous Cycle of Learning, Growing, and Overcoming

At the heart of the warrior's journey is the recognition that personal development is an endless cycle—a spiral of experiences that continually shape and refine our essence.

The Journey of Lifelong Learning: This journey underscores the importance of remaining lifelong learners, ever curious and open to the lessons that life presents. Each day offers a fresh canvas for exploration, discovery, and the expansion of our understanding. By fostering a mindset of perpetual learning, we ensure that our journey is marked by continuous evolution and enlightenment.

Embracing Growth Through Every Challenge: The path of growth is often paved with challenges, each serving as a crucible for our development. Sun Tzu's strategies teach us to face these challenges with grace and strategic acumen, extracting wisdom and strength from every encounter. It is through the process of overcoming that we carve out our path to self-discovery, learning to wield our struggles as tools for our transformation.

The Spiral of Self-Discovery and Renewal: As we navigate the cycle of learning and growth, we venture deeper into the spiral of self-discovery, each loop bringing us closer to our core self while propelling us into new realms of understanding and being. This spiral is not just a journey inward but a process of renewal, where each cycle sheds old layers, revealing the luminescence of our true nature.

The warrior's journey to self-discovery and recovery is a testament to the resilience of the human spirit, a reminder that within each of us lies the potential to transcend our limitations and emerge victorious. By weaving the strategic insights of Sun Tzu into the narrative of our lives, we equip ourselves with the tools necessary to navigate the complexities of existence with grace, purpose, and unwavering determination. As we tread this endless path, let us carry the torch of our learnings, illuminating the way for others, as we continue to learn, grow, and overcome, in an eternal dance of self-revelation and renewal.

Made in United States
Troutdale, OR
08/24/2024

22274227R00119